Testimonials

"I have been coming to Karen's classes for over a year now as I think they're fantastic! Having been to similar outdoor boot camps before where I didn't feel challenged or motivated, I soon learned this is not something lacking in Karen's classes! I used her workouts to strengthen and tone alongside my marathon training, and I credit these for keeping me injury free throughout. Her energy is infectious, despite working hard I still find it fun, and she adapts the exercises for all fitness levels so each person is working to the best of their ability." - Helen Gilbert

"Training with Karen makes me feel strong and fit. Her positive and non judgemental attitude keeps me going. I actually look forward to going to bootcamp; it's such a great start to the day. Doing Karen's workouts have helped me to feel confident with my body. She has a no nonsense approach that truly makes sense and feels achievable. Karen loves what she does and is a fantastic motivator. I can't thank her enough!" - Katharine Alexandra Doll

"Karen is vibrant and energetic. Her presence alone motivates anyone into wanting to strive for the best. Karen is inspirational, and engages your mind, body and soul. She listens to your needs and shows you how to work hard in getting there. Not only is she a personal trainer but she becomes a friend, she listens to you, and every session you come out feeling a better version of yourself. She is a true warrior and is a prime example showing the world that we can achieve anything if we put our minds to it. Not only does Karen teach me how to get fit, she teaches you how to remain positive, how to eat healthy, and how to fit fitness into your everyday life. Training with Karen is fun, I look forward to my sessions with her and I believe in her because she believes in me." - Yazmin Layla Rose

"Karen is not only my personal trainer, but the most positive and inspiring person I have ever met! Karen's amazing outlook on life and determination to see the good in everyone and everything is what makes her so special. Not only does she inspire me to be fit and healthy, she encourages me to remain positive and appreciate all the good things in life. Karen listens to what you want to achieve and what you want to get out of your sessions and every week delivers something different and fun. Her energy and presence alone are enough to make you feel refreshed and I look forward to seeing her every week. Her passion for what she does is so uplifting and I truly believe that everyone needs a Karen in their life!" - Georgia Johnson

"I have been training with Karen for over 3 years now and can honestly say I would never go back to my previous lifestyle. I was lucky enough to meet Karen through a boot camp 3 years ago and it has made such a difference to my body. I remember my first training session with Karen and I thought to myself "never again" and I would find excuses not to exercise, but Karen pushed me to carry on and I'm so glad I did because today "I feel amazing". Karen is very focused, committed and has a positive mind-set and has inspired me to live a healthier lifestyle and has encouraged me to exercise. Not only is Karen one of the best personal trainers I have come across she is also a great mentor. I'm so happy our paths crossed. - Suki Panessar

"I joined Karen's bootcamp as I had a couple of stone to shed after pregnancy. I was frustrated at how difficult it was to lose the weight and felt like giving up but Karen's positive attitude spurred me on. Every week is hard work but fun and she mixes the exercises up so there is no chance of getting bored. Karen also gave me an eating plan which suits me perfectly and I can see and feel the weight dropping off. Karen has made me feel fitter, happier, and a lot more confident and I actually love myself again. I am so glad I signed up to a new lease of life." - Zoe Mellors

"Karen is quite simply a breath of fresh air. After many years of trying different diets/eating plans and exercise programmes I have finally found one that works and it's all thanks to Karen! She is a fantastic trainer, so encouraging, inspiring and realistic which is so important. I feel so much happier and I'm now well on my way to achieving my own personal goal and with Karen's support I know I will definitely get there!" - Jo Adams

"Just to say I am so, so, so pleased with Karen and all she's done and keeps doing with me she is a true inspiration. I am not the average client by a long shot. My aim wasn't the usual bootcamp aim but one to try to keep a healthy lifestyle and stay fit and active. This is not always easy due to my heart condition but even on my really crap days when we just get out and walk Karen makes me feel like I have achieved gold. Karen's made me believe in myself and that I can do things, maybe not as I did but adapt in another way. This weekend on Saturday night I walked 15 miles around London on the moon walk for breast cancer in my ridiculous decorated bra. It wasn't easy by a long shot and very cold but I kept going with the aid of the team supporting me, family, son, daughter and special friends who believe in me, also with Karen's voice in my head - you can do anything you put your mind too Alison you're amazing!!! When my body has recovered I hope to achieve much more. A Fantastic inspirational person in every way. - Alison Kirkbright

Supporters

Kam Winchester
Acupuncture in Eden
www.acupunctureineden.co.uk
acupunctureineden@gmail.com
07861 216992
Acupuncture can help you lose weight alongside your journey, to becoming a healthier you.

Rebecca Hirst
Glorious Wellness
www.gloriouswellness.com
rebecca@gloriouswellness.co.uk
07792 649934
Nutrition coach. Wellness expert. TEDx speaker. Helping busy people to feel gloriously well.

Lorraine Biggs
Lorraine M. Biggs
www.lorrainembiggs.co.uk
lorrainembiggs@gmail.com
07979 478874
Empowering women with a brief, gentle mind/body process.

THERA P
Massage & sports injury clinic www.thera-p.co.uk
info@thera-p.co.uk
07594 216091
Clinic offering faster recovery, injury prevention and peak performance advice.

Lee & Sarah Chapman
Ripped Muscle & Fitness Ltd
www.rippedmuscleandfitnessltd.co.uk
rippedmuscleandfitness@yahoo.com
01689 874579
Friendly family run gym that can help you reach your goals.

Contents

Acknowledgements

Thank you to my amazing three children Kieron, Robyn and Millie you have been my drive, my push, my absolute desire to keep going no matter how tough life has been. Your support has meant so much to me. I love you all from the bottom of my heart and wouldn't be the capable woman I am today without you all by my side. You are the making of me each of you in turn has brought some special meaning to my life. I'm super proud of you all.

Thank you to John Foti for having belief when I was so unsure of myself and my capability in passing my exams to become a PT. Your encouragement and guidance will stay with me always. My fitness career very much all started with you.

Thank you Daniel Welstead. You have been a great teacher a true leader. I will never forget your answer when I told you that, if I'm half as good as you I will be very happy with myself - Your response I want you to be better. Your words of encouragement have pushed me beyond my own boundaries of what I've felt I'm capable of. You're a true gentleman. You proved to me without doubt there are some great men out there.

Thank you to all my wonderful clients it's been a pleasure to work with each and every one of you.

Thank you Rosemary Hull one of the wisest women I have known.

Thank you Aly Harrold for working your public speaking magic on me.

Thank you Sharon Lynn and Lorenzo Guescini for working your book writing magic on me.

Thank you to my parents Linda and Bob, to all my family and friends for supporting me through the years and very much contributing to helping me to get where I am today.

Thank you to those people who haven't made my life easy because you unknowingly made me stronger.

PART ONE

1

It's Your Choice

"The only thing standing between you and the body you want is you; and the choices you make."

A 2001 magazine claimed that of all the British women who completed their survey, only 10% were happy with their bodies. A massive 90% were not. For the majority of those women, weight was the issue and two thirds of them admitted they would consider resorting to cosmetic surgery to change what made them unhappy about their bodies. Can you relate to this? Or do you know of someone that can? It was after reading those statistics that I felt compelled to write a book. I have since discovered that this is not just an issue here in the UK. According to a survey online carried out by Dove, it is at a critical level on a global scale. I am also confident that it isn't just the women of the world that are feeling this way. Both women and men are under increasing pressure from advertising and media to reach an unrealistic standard of beauty, which is the key force in driving appearance anxiety.

If you have picked up this book and you are happy with your body; congratulations! You're one of the 10% that are with me. My goal is to turn that 90% figure on its head. I want 90% of women to be happy in their own bodies. The reason I want to do this is because I was once one of those unhappy women. I now have over thirty three years' worth of weight gain and loss experience under my belt and I am no longer part of that 90%. I know how it feels to be both four stone overweight and two stone underweight. I've hated my body; I've loathed exercise and the thought of doing it. I've been young and very unfit and unhealthy. Through the power of choice, I have now turned all of this around. I love my body. I love exercise and the thought of doing it most of the time. Having the body I always wanted was in my control all along. Making different life choices has enabled me to achieve this, as well as cultivating a great career in fitness. I am now the 'me' I've always wanted to be. If I can do it, I can show you how to do it too. My life has not been easy but I firmly believe that the people who have been through the most are the best people to help others. I've had to go through tough times so that you don't have to.

I attended a book writing course and was advised to get specific about my reader as it really helps to have a person in mind when you are writing. Hindsight is a wonderful thing, so the person I thought about was me. This is the book I wish my sixteen year old self could have read when she was unhappy with her body. This book is filled with advice I wish I had known. If only I'd known then what I know now. I would have made much better choices for sure. But there is no point in having regrets in life. You cannot change the past. What you can do though, with knowledge, is make better choices from the start. In the next chapter, I will talk you through how making the right choices has enabled me not only to get the happy body I always wanted but also a career I absolutely love.

2
It's Never Too Late!

Let's start at the beginning of my fat to fitness and ultimate happiness journey. My name is Karen Jones and I am a mother of three children whose ages range from thirteen to thirty two. My main job is as a fitness trainer but I am also a bootcamp instructor, power yoga teacher, bikini fitness athlete and public speaker. On top of all this, I am now an author of my first fitness/wellness book.

YAY.

I was born on April 7th 1968 which makes me forty nine years old by the time this book is published. I can tell you hand on heart that I feel ageless and so full of energy and happiness, thanks to fitness and all that it brings. I'm not one of the lucky ones that was born this way. I have not always been a healthy weight with an athletic body. I wish...

To achieve the body I've always wanted I've had to work hard for it. My biggest weight gain happened after the birth of my first child way back in 1984 when I was just sixteen years old and not long left school. I had put on a massive four stone in weight post baby. It was back in the days when you were told to eat for two and I took that quite literally and ate for three. I had a craving for chocolate or that's what I told myself back then. As a result, a lot of chocolate was consumed. I remember standing there in my knickers and bra staring at my post baby body reflection in the mirror. Staring back at me was my chubby face and I looked down to see my fat thighs touching. My big belly and hips were covered in stretch marks and my boobs were huge. I felt fat, unhappy and ugly. I hated my body. I lost that excess weight within a year by literally starving myself. I lived on just black coffee, cigarettes and very little food. I really didn't know any better.

I was living on my own with my son in a hostel at the time and dropped down to around seven and a half stone. It wasn't until my mum said to me one day on visiting her that I was looking way too thin that I took control and stopped. I had a baby to take care of now, I needed to be responsible and look after him by taking care of me.

Looking back, I would say I had developed an eating disorder. Thankfully, I pulled back from this without medical intervention. I spent many years after this yo-yo dieting, never really finding a diet that worked for me long term. I tried every diet under the sun and NONE of them ever worked for me long term. For years and years I'd lose weight and then put it straight back on, driving myself quite literally mad. Sound familiar?

By the time I was thirty six, I'd had two more babies and found myself suffering from the baby blues for the first time around four months post my last pregnancy. When I explained how I felt to my health visitor on a home visit, she said to me I had one of two choices; I could go see my doctor and be prescribed anti-depressants or I could take up exercise as this was known to help. After some thought, I chose exercise. At that time, the nearest gym to me was a good thirty minutes' drive away from where I lived; there and back was an hour out of my day. Being a mother your time is precious and you need something that is time effective. Exercising for an hour would make more sense than driving for an hour, right? So I asked myself what I could do that was on my doorstep. With this firmly in my mind, the answer came to me... RUNNING.

Off I went - I started slow using a run walk program that I came up with myself. In just over a year I got myself up to running non-stop for around half an hour a couple of times a week. I went from not really liking or enjoying running or exercising to loving it over time. All was good until my grandad Ron fell ill and in a relatively short time died. He had prostate cancer, although this illness may not have killed him. I felt sad about his passing and the pain I know he suffered towards the end of his days. I began to feel myself feeling down again, as you do when you lose a loved one. Around this time, I picked up a London marathon magazine in a sports shop.

It read; 'If you can run comfortably now for half an hour, you're capable of running the marathon in April next year.' I thought to myself, I can do that! I decided to run for a cancer charity on behalf of my grandads memory and raise money to try to cure this terrible illness that takes away our loved ones before their time. So that's what I did. Unfortunately, I'd also lost my nan Irene, grandad Ron's wife to cancer way before her time. Cancer sucks. I wanted to turn my negative feelings into positive ones. It's not easy getting into running the London marathon first time but I did it; I found a way and made it happen. I self-trained for several months and on the 23rd April 2006 I ran in my first ever adult race. It was tough. A lot tougher than I had ever imagined and I must confess I did power walk the last few miles coming in, finally crossing that finish line at 5.20hrs. I was a little disappointed in my time until I found out that Steve Redgrave, an Olympic athlete came in 9 minutes after me.

Although it didn't feel like it at the time of finishing, it was one of the best days of my life. Definitely one of the most monumental days and a very big turning point for me. I learnt something that day when I crossed the finish line that changed me and my outlook on life forever. I will explain more about this further on in the book. One thing is for sure; completing that marathon helped me to become the strong, capable, determined, independent woman I am today. Running that marathon helped me realise that at the age of thirty eight, I had not only overcome the baby blues but also lost and kept the weight off; simply by eating healthily and exercising. I felt great, looked great and had so much more extra energy to run around after my children. The big secret in life is you have to spend energy to get energy! I had finally got off that yo-yo dieting merry go round.

For the next five years I kept up my running, fitness and healthy eating. I had found something that worked for me. I had learnt one of the most important things a woman can master in her life; to love your body. I did and I loved being me. I absolutely loved exercise. It was around this period of self-discovery that my unhappy, toxic marriage broke down. The next year was the worst of my life as I went through a horrendous divorce. Thankfully I used exercise as my stress release. Fitness kept me mentally and physically strong and for the most part sane!

I'd been a stay at home mother for sixteen years since my middle child Robyn had come along. My youngest child Millie by that time was seven years old. My solicitors told me I'd have to retrain for a career. I had to think hard about what I'd love to do for the rest of my working life.

I soon whittled it down to two options; Interior designer or fitness trainer. One of my best friends Alison was an interior designer and told me that she worked unsociable hours and most weekends. That wasn't going to work for me. I wanted to be with my children and also if I had to factor in childcare costs I probably wouldn't earn very much either. A career in fitness seemed to be the right choice and career path for me. It was one I knew I would love and feel most passionate about. I imagined myself doing this work at fifty (I was forty four at the time) sixty, even seventy. I thought to myself I can also keep fit along the way. I would just evolve and work hard at a career I loved. If I worked with mothers, I knew I'd work mostly school hours and not weekends as they wouldn't want me to come at these times. Bingo, happy working days.

I went on an intensive course, qualified as a level 2 Gym Instructor and then on to a level 3 Personal Trainer. I met some great people on my course; I loved every moment of doing it. To think I was worried I wouldn't do well as it had been many years since I'd been to school. The thought of exams scared the hell out of me, but to my absolute delight, I passed both of the exams. As you can imagine I was so completely chuffed with myself. My teacher John said I went from the bottom of the class to nearly the top with my sheer determination to pass my exams.

I knew from the off I didn't want to work in a gym. I had the most empathy and connection with mothers so I wanted to train them at home. I felt I could offer my knowledge and expertise to other mothers as I had experienced these things myself. I understood the daily struggle of looking after yourself as well as looking after your family. The thing I came to realise over time is the more you look after yourself as a mother, the more you have to give others and the better quality that giving will be. Help yourself first to help others after. A good example is how, on a airplane, they tell you to put your own oxygen mask on before helping anybody else.

I started out training mothers one to one in their own homes. I soon became comfortable with that and wanted to move on to training people in groups. A very good friend of mine Sarah introduced me to Daniel Welstead, an amazing fitness man who owned his own bootcamp company. It just so happened that Daniel was looking for a female personal trainer who he could teach to run his beginners bootcamp. I was going to be that woman. I was trained up by him to become a bootcamp instructor.

There's a You Tube clip out there somewhere proving just that, ha-ha.... I love teaching people how to exercise safely and effectively. I have the most patience; I really come into my own. It's wonderful for me to see the progression my clients make from beginner to intermediate to advanced. As I was very much a beginner once, myself. Remember this whenever you're starting something new. Every single expert starts out as a beginner. There's no shame and everyone loves a trier, they really do. Just start and keep going and you'll be an expert in no time. My uncle Martin once told me it's NEVER too late to change, and he was right. That advice has helped me massively over the years since I received it twenty years ago. Thank you Uncle Martin! It's funny how certain words stay firmly in your mind, how one sentence can have such a profound positive effect on your life.

I now specialise in home fitness training after taking part in a UKBFF Ultimate Beginners Bikini fitness contest in July 2015 at the age of forty seven. I wanted to show women of all ages that you do not need a gym to get a good body. I home trained mostly, not touching a gym to get my body ready for that contest. I followed a healthy eating plan and exercised most days, for seven months. I achieved the body you can see on the back of this book. I had a second Caesarean section with my third child and was told by a doctor that one of the downsides of having a second C-section was that I wouldn't have a flat stomach again. With exercise I proved you can.

I found on the day of the contest that I had just as good a body as the other contestants in my category, and to my knowledge they had all worked out in gyms. I think this proves that by using your own body weight and very little equipment, you can still achieve a great body outside of the gym. Many of my clients, both women and men, come to me to get fit because they do not want to go to the gym. It's not that I'm against gym fitness. I just wanted to show there is another way.

It's whatever works best for the individual. I would go outside for cardio training like running or power walking, and I'd also take part in outdoor bootcamps. I used a set of dumbbells at home, along with a swiss ball, medicine ball and towards the last two months of training I also purchased a weighted bar. I then took up yoga; it just made good sense to me to condition the muscle I was building up. I knew I wanted to look lean and conditioned but I didn't realise taking up yoga would bring me so much more. Not only am I more flexible, my body is stronger and my mind is at peace. Yoga has become an integral part of my workout regime. I'm so happy I discovered yoga at this time in my life. I cannot recommend and promote it enough as there are so many benefits of taking it up. It's a beautiful exercise; it slows everything down and stretches everything out. I love it. I love teaching it too; it's another string to my exercise bow.

3

Change Happens

I LOVE, LOVE, LOVE, EXERCISE AND HEALTHY EATING.

The last eleven years have shown me so many benefits, and it all started when I took up running! I now have a successful fitness career off the back of taking up exercise. I also have my own bootcamp company named Mad Mothers Bootcamp. (In writing this book, my bootcamp name has changed to Happy You, Happy Body Bootcamp*.) My main goal in life is to help people get fit. It's crazy how one career path has taken me down another; for instance, I soon discovered I could talk fitness and exercise all day long which is why I've now gone into public speaking. I went into public speaking so I can reach an even bigger audience and spread the fitness word. I hope, just from reading this book that you can see how passionate I am about my work. I'm also passionate about helping people to live happy, long, active lives. It was while doing the research for my public speaking course where I made the discovery of the statistics I mentioned at the beginning of this book. I first used those figures during a talk on 10th December 2016 and I am still determined to turn that figure on its head. I felt whole heartedly that the best way for me to do that was to write a book to show you how I did it.

Not everyone is concerned with having a bikini fit body, I know that. That bikini contest was a stepping stone for me; it gave me more knowledge and experience that helped me further my career and get me to where I wanted to be. This extra knowledge and experience would also help me to serve my clients more effectively, as it was my job to help them get the fit, healthy, happy body that they want.

This book isn't about getting you a perfect body. It's about giving you the tools to acquire the perfect body for you. It's important for you to be as GOOD AS YOU CAN BE.

If I can go from hating my body as a teenage mother to loving my body as a woman, through exercising, nourishing and looking after myself, then so can you. So, let's do this shall we? We can do this together, with my love and support. I shall hold your hand all the way through this journey. I have been told if I could bottle my energy and happiness I'd be wealthy. I am already wealthy in family, knowledge, good health and happiness. I can't bottle up everything I have, but I can put all of my energy and happiness into this book; they say those things are contagious, and I believe that it's true.

*The original name for my book was Mad Mothers Mission but I came to the realisation that the title wasn't portraying the message that I wanted it to. I want all readers of the world, both men and women to pick up and read my book, not just mothers. With the original title I'm not sure men would feel it was for them. I want to be known as the happy body creator and my mission to create healthy, happy bodies is paramount to me. For that reason, I have chosen a new tittle; I've gone from Mad Mothers Mission to Happy You, Happy Body. I love this new title and it proves that at any moment you can choose to make changes in your life when and as you choose to do so. It's your life...The key to your success is to embrace change and be open to change.

4

The Happy Body Solution

I don't have a magic wand; I cannot magically wave it for you to gain the body you want. You're going to have to take ownership of this yourself. Accept that you are beautiful just the way you are. Work hard and become your own hero/heroine in your life story.

Just as I have had to find a way that works best for me, all I can do is supply you with all the ingredients that you need to make the right choices to attain the body you have always wanted. You must take control over your own mind and body to find out what works best for you. We are all very much unique. It is NOT one size fits all.

The following chapter headings in this book spell out the word **MENTAL**.

M is for Mind

E is for Emotions

N is for Nutrition

T is for Training

A is for Attire

L is for Longevity

Mind - because I believe that is where it all starts. You must get your mind in the right place first.

Emotions - the most important of which are self-love and acceptance.

Nutrition - 80% of this journey is down to diet, my friends. You've got to get your diet right.

Training - the good news is it's only 20% exercise.

Attire - active wear and wearing the right gear.

Longevity - why is healthy eating and fitness important? For me personally it is so I'm comfortable in my own skin. I want to feel great and look great. I want to stay as young as I can for as long as I can and to live a happy, long, healthy life. I want to feel the best that I can. I want to be happy with what God has given me by loving and respecting my body. I want to be a happy and healthy ME.

This journey is designed to last your whole life; it is not a short term fix. I really do see the big picture. I know my future self will thank me for all the effort I have put into myself now, when it counts the most. That goes for you too...

PART TWO

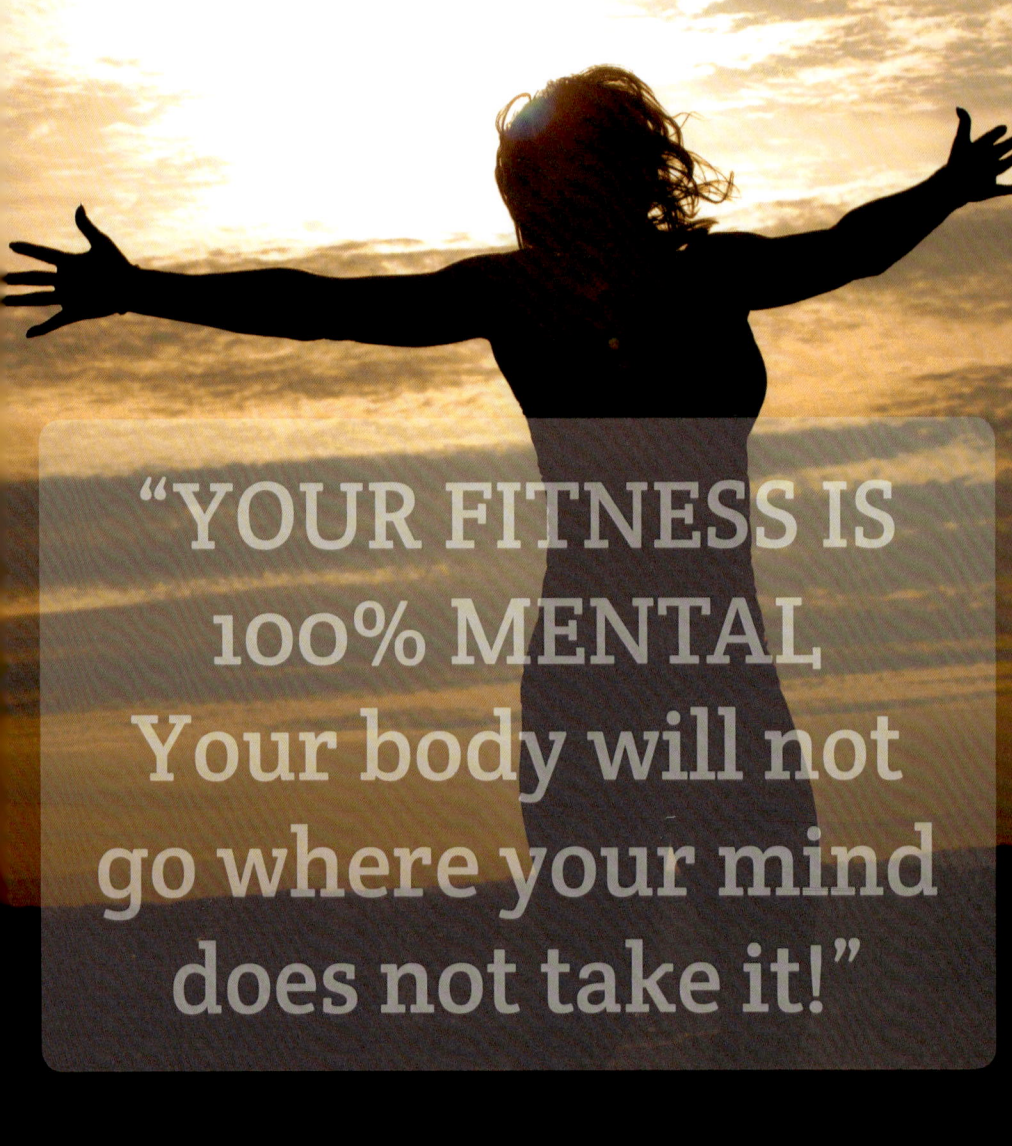

"YOUR FITNESS IS 100% MENTAL Your body will not go where your mind does not take it!"

5

Mind

You might think that your mind has nothing to do with the body that you want, but trust me, the mind means EVERYTHING. My body transformation started with my mind. Your thoughts become your reality.

People say I make it look easy when I demonstrate an exercise or when I talk to them about weight loss, and it is easy when you know how. Any expert can make what they do sound easy, because they do the same thing over and over again. As I wrote earlier in the book though, every expert starts out as a beginner. We've all got to start somewhere. I have set out to write this book in a logical order of what needs to come first, and this is why I've started with the mind.

You become what you tell yourself to become. Your mind is always listening, so whether you're discussing your body with your family or with friends, or even just thinking internally in your own mind, make sure you always speak kindly of yourself and of others too, come to that.

I once read a statement which I believe to be true; 'It's all in your mind. Whatever you hold in your mind will tend to occur in your life. If you continue to believe as you have always believed, you will continue to act as you have always acted. If you continue to act as you have always acted, you will continue to get what you have always gotten. If you want different results in your life or your work, all you have to do is change your mind.' - Anonymous.

I'm sure you have all heard the saying that insanity is doing the same thing over and over and expecting different results. It's true! You must change your mind set first and then your actions will follow.

On the flip side of that, once you find what works for you, you must keep doing it :) I found what works for me and I continually do the same thing, every day, every week, every month and every year, which is why I have stayed the same weight for over a decade now. Your desire for change must be stronger than your desire to stay the same. It's as simple as that. Your aim should be to get the body you want by remaining as healthy as possible while achieving it. Your mind must stay strong for you to achieve the body you have always wanted, along with your weight loss and fitness goals. You must hold those goals strongly in your mind and work out the best way to achieve them.

You are the creator of your own thoughts; this is something I have had to master and something I think is important for you too. In a second you can change your mind from negative to positive and vice versa. There are usually two battles going on in your head about how you want to be. Your positive voice of reason will want one thing and your negative voice of doubt will want another. Your positive self-talk will want to implement the changes you desire and the negative thoughts will want you to stay the same. Only you choose which one will win.

Just as you can train your muscles to be stronger, you can train your brain to think more positively and quieten your negative self-talk so you hear less of that and more of the positive thoughts. It just takes practice and repetition. If you catch yourself thinking negative thoughts you must change them straight away back to positive. Some people think they have no control over their mind. You do.

People always comment on how positive I am and the reason for that is because I simply tell myself that I am. I have not always had a lot of willpower but I have now trained my mind to tell my body that I do, so it is easier now than it used to be.

To explain what I mean by this, I would like to use another quote; 'Whether you think you can or whether you think you can't, you're usually right.' How many times has somebody told you they have no willpower? I once thought I had no willpower because I smoked, I drank in excess and I ate all the wrong, unhealthy foods. I did a lot of things I probably shouldn't have because I believed I couldn't change as I possessed no self-control or will power. Eventually, I took back my control and willpower and changed the way I was living. If I can do it, so can you.

Many of you will be focusing on the negatives in your life that you want to change, but you need to flip this into a positive. For example;

"I don't want to be fat" becomes *"I want to be a healthy weight."*

"I don't want to be unhealthy" becomes *"I want to be healthy."*

"I don't want to be ill" becomes *"I want to be well."*

"I don't have any willpower" becomes *"I have lots of willpower."*

"I have no self-control" becomes *"I have lots of self-control."*

"I have no self-discipline" becomes *"I have lots of self-discipline."*

Affirmations are your conscious thoughts which in turn become your reality. They are short powerful statements. Affirmations are a great way to fill your mind with positive thoughts. Always focus on what you want, not what you don't want. You may not believe yourself when you first start out telling yourself your positive affirmations, but trust me; it won't take long before you start becoming exactly what you think. Within reason of course. How awesome is that? It's all completely in your power. You have just got to believe it.

'I am' are two of the most powerful words you can say to yourself so be sure your 'I am' is followed by a positive affirmation of yourself. Some of my positive affirmations are: I am happy. I am healthy. I am a perfect weight for me. I am confident. I am attractive. I am positive. I am ageless. I am strong. I am determined. I am loving. I am kind. I am smart. I am dedicated. I am persistent. I am whatever I choose to be. Get the picture?

In time, you really will become what you think. When I hear my clients being negative about themselves, I tell them to stop and repeat back the negative thoughts. We then flip it into a positive affirmation. We have an inbuilt safety mechanism that wants us to stay the same. We actually fear change, so I use a simple strategy whenever I want to change or achieve something in my life.

Think it - Believe it - Action it.

Think it – I decide on exactly what it is that I want so my intention is fully formed.

Believe it - I visualise what I want and imagine that I already have it or have already achieved it.

Action it - I take the action to get whatever it is that I want.

A lot of people know in their mind that they want to change and this is called contemplation. You can be in this state of mind for a very long time. You know you want to be healthier and slimmer; you are just not sure how that change must come about.

The best way for it to come about is to be clear in your mind as to what it is you want and how you want your healthy body to be, look and feel. You can never go back; you can only ever be a new version of you. I work with clients that will say they used to have a great body, for example before they had children. My response is always to tell them that there is nothing stopping them from having a great or even better body than what they had before. Take me for instance; my body is better now after three children than it was after my first child at sixteen. You just have to believe that's possible and work at it. I used to listen to women who said that they felt better than they did in their early twenties and I never believed them. Now, I know that it is true because as I am approaching fifty, that is how I feel. I had to see it with my own eyes to believe it. If this is not how you feel, check to see what you are telling yourself.

Healthy eating and exercise is the answer. We live in a society where we want everything instantly. I believe if you earn it, you appreciate it more. It took me seven months to get a bikini fit body and as I worked out, I always kept my eye on the end goal. There were many days where I couldn't feel a difference or see a change, but I had to believe it was happening; otherwise I am sure I would have given up. This is how you will feel many times yourself during your transformational period. Keep going. Make it happen! Do not take your eye off that end goal.

I discovered that in order for change to happen, you had to get uncomfortable, and you will come to recognise that too. In exercise, most people will stop when the burn happens in their muscles, which is when the lactic acid builds up due to the exertion. You must push through the burn for the change to happen. I tell my clients to embrace that burn, to treat that as your friend because that's where the biggest change happens. You must breathe through the burn; reframe it in your mind and think of it as happy pain. The pain must happen for the gain to occur. Muhammad Ali didn't start counting until that burn kicked in because he knew that there was no gain without pain. Learn to love that muscle burn. As in life, most people stop something when it becomes uncomfortable. They stop what they are doing and revert back to their old ways staying safe, when to experience the change they desire, they must keep going.

A very common example is the resolutions people make for a new year. Many people join a gym because they have decided they would like to lose weight and become healthier; they have very good intentions. But by the end of January, beginning of February, many of those same people have given up because it seems like too much hard work and it hurts; their bodies ache and their muscles are sore. If only they pushed through the next month or two they would start seeing and feeling the results they were after, but unfortunately most give in.

Greatness takes time – I once read that it takes thirteen hours to build a Toyota and six months to build a Rolls Royce. I know which one I'd rather be. It can take up to one month for you to notice your body changing. Then two months for your friends to notice a difference in you. At three months, everybody else will notice the difference in you too. Keep going at it! I have embraced change many times in my life. I now find it easy to recognise when I am going through the difficult, uncomfortable bit. I may cry during this time and hate whatever it is that I have to do, but I both mentally and physically push through. I make it happen by continually pushing through. Your body can go on for much longer than the mind thinks it can.

Weight loss seems to be the main cause of why so many women are unhappy with their bodies but health is much more important than just weight alone. Too many women are striving for an unrealistic target on the scales that they never seem to be able to reach and it is this that is making them miserable and unhappy.

YOU ARE THE ONLY PERSON WHO KNOWS HOW MUCH YOU WEIGH.

There were times in my life when I wanted to be eight and a half stone but I now know that that weight is not a comfortable, sustainable weight for me to sit at. I would have hardly any fat on me and I have actually learned to love my curves. In my opinion, curves are sexy. Only twice in these ten years have I dropped weight and both were during testing periods of my life. The first time was when I was going through my divorce; I literally had to feed myself up to stay a healthy weight. When you go through a testing time and you're running on adrenaline, you tend to lose weight really easy. You need your strength and a crystal clear mind, so make sure you eat. Your brain is the first organ to be effected when you're hungry. You need food for brain energy and thinking power. I believe you put good things in to you to get good things out.

The second time I lost weight was when I was training for the bikini fitness contest. I was working out so much that again I had to feed myself up to stay my healthy weight. I had to lose a stone in weight, approximately 6 kilos over the last few weeks of training because my posing coach, Sarah Bridges, said my legs were out of proportion with the rest of my body. I followed a strict eating plan which consisted of eating every 3-4 hours starting at 7am each day. My last meal of the day was at 10pm. On top of this, I drank a gallon of Evian water and did three hours of cardio every day. I did lose that stone in weight but some people thought I looked way too slim. I lost that weight because I'd entered a contest. Sarah my posing coach is an IBFF pro; a British Champion body builder herself and a EFBB judge. She is an expert at what she does; I paid for her advice and so took it on board. I couldn't wait to put the weight back on after the contest, for reasons I will explain in detail further along.

I know if I drop below 58 kilos my clothes feel too loose on me and if I go up above 62 kilos they get uncomfortably tight, so I use this as my gauge. I sit very happily between a UK sizes 10 to 12. I promised myself a long time ago that I would never again be bigger than a size twelve or smaller than a size ten, that way I don't keep having to replace my clothes, and the same clothes fit me year in, year out. I have some items of clothes in my wardrobe that are over ten years old and still look good on me. I don't tend to follow fashion trends but instead buy clothes that suit my body shape and fit me well. I aim for stylish, smart and chic so that I look timeless and not out of date with fashion. I might then add one or two pieces from current fashion trends. I find this means I don't have to keep clothes shopping, therefore saving time and money. I love my clothes.

How did I find the perfect weight for me? On a BMI scale for my age, height and weight, I sit quite happily in the centre slightly over to the right. The same as in the height/ weight chart I share with you (see Figure 1). I'm very happy about this. I know if I drop weight too much as I had to do in my bikini fitness contest, the weight doesn't always come off exactly where you want it to. It comes off in areas that you do not want it to come off, which can cause problems. For example, if you lose weight on your face, it will make you look older and people will remark that you look ill which is never a good look. It will also come off your boobs. Huff. There are downsides to being underweight and some of the women I know who are underweight wish that they could put weight on. Fancy that; it works both ways.

After I had taken part in the contest, I couldn't wait to feed myself back up to my healthy perfect weight again. I wanted my face to fill out and to get my boobs back. I can tell you, I'd rather be a little overweight than a little under. Let your clothes and how you feel and look be your main guide. Do not be under any pressure from looking at unrealistic body images in magazines or in the media; they are not real life. My contest bikini no longer fits me and I honestly don't mind. A lot of women think that getting to their goal weight will make them happy. Why wait until then? Be happy now. Hand on heart, I didn't feel any happier when I had lost that stone in weight. It's all in your head. Flick that switch and change that thought.

To get the body you want, you have to be clear on what your goals are. For instance, if you want to lose weight, then your goal has to be very specific. What weight do you want to be? First, you have to decide on a healthy weight for you. Just because some people are slim, doesn't mean they are healthy, and just because someone is bigger, it doesn't mean they are unhealthy either. Health is the most important thing here; it has to be your main concern. So how do you determine if you are a healthy weight?

It is common knowledge that if you are overweight you are more at risk of health problems such as heart disease, type 2 diabetes and certain cancers.

One way you can keep an eye on whether you are a healthy weight or not is to check your BMI (Body Mass Index). This is a measure that uses your height and weight to work out if your weight is healthy.

BMI is also calculated using your gender and age. There are a number of websites and phone apps that will allow you to calculate this for yourself; there are even high tech scales that you can use at home for this too. Some will even tell you how hydrated you are (or not) which is equally important to know.

(Personally, I use the free app from NHS Choices) You can have a healthy BMI but still have excess belly fat. I have found that the belly area is the most problematic area where my clients carry excess weight. To remain healthy, you should try to lose weight from this area - regardless of your height or BMI.

So how do you know if you have excess belly fat?

Here's how to measure your waist effectively: Find the bottom of your ribs and the top of your hips; midway between these points is the waist. Grab a tape measure and wrap the tape around your waist. Breathe out naturally before taking this measurement.

If you are over these measurements, you should try to lose weight;

94cm (37ins) for men

80cm (31.5ins) for women

You are at significantly higher risk, and should contact your GP, if your waist is: 102cm (40ins) or more for men

88cm (34ins) or more for women

Figure 1. is a height/weight guide from NHS Choices website, these are guides and in some cases not relevant. For instance, people who do sports that bulk them up. If you're concerned, it may be a good idea to go and see your doctor.

Not everyone works by scales or even wants to weigh themselves. Some people are happy to go by their clothes size. You must do whatever works for you. Bodies come in all shapes and sizes, and as I've said and will say again, it is health over weight. The important thing for you is to be whatever weight you want to be, as long as you are healthy. Do not go by what your mother, lover, brother, aunt, cousin, friend or foe wants for you to be. You be what you want. It's your life and your body. Just please, please be healthy. That should always be your top priority.

Figure 1.

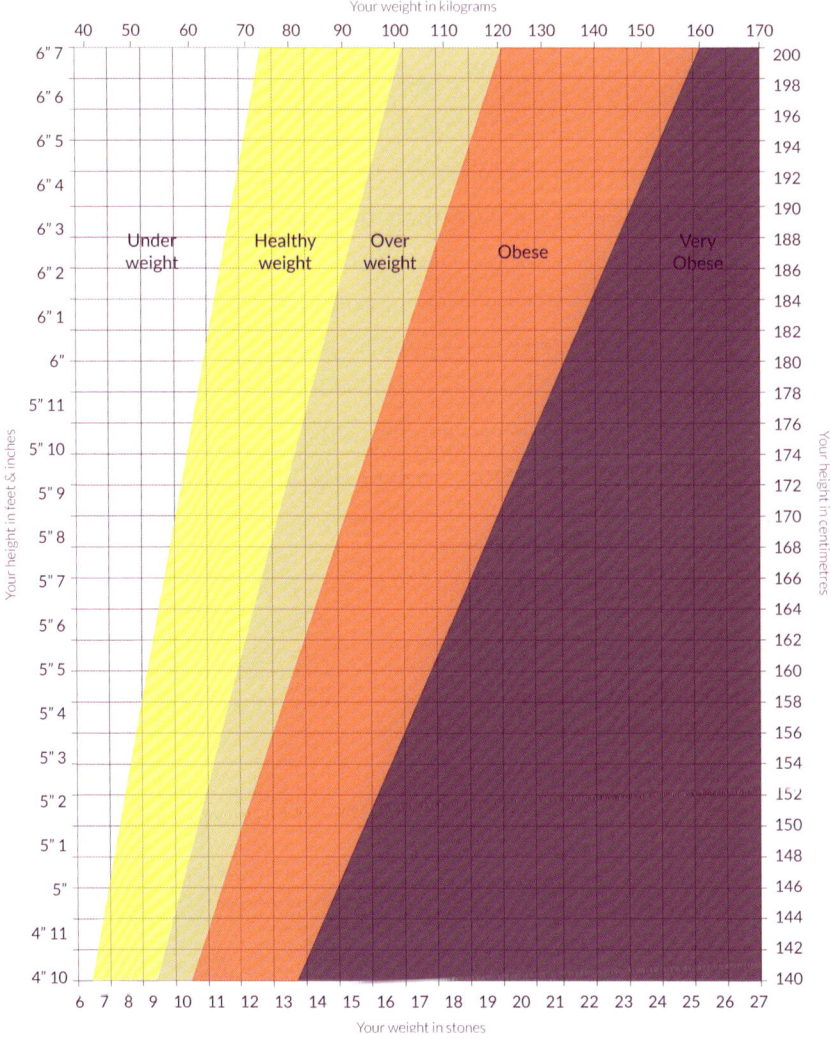

When I was younger, I realised there is no point being slim and unhealthy. There's no point at all. The same is on the flip side of that. There is no point in being bigger and unhealthy. You must find a weight that is healthy and makes you feel happy.

Government guidelines say that a healthy weight loss per week is one to two pounds or 0.5 to 1 kilos approx. This is the advice I give my clients once I have done a BMI reading and taken their body measurements. It's good to do body measurements as well (This is because you don't always see the numbers on the scale going down but you do see inch loss.) We then discuss a realistic weight for them to aim for. We work out how much weight they want to lose then divide that by weeks to see approximately how long it will take them to achieve that weight loss goal. As you go down in weight you should keep checking how you feel in your clothes; you may not need to drop as much weight as you think. It's your own personal goal and you may find you feel happier sitting at a bigger size.

Have you heard of **SMART** goals?

This stands for;

S – Specific

M – Measurable

A - Achievable

R - Relevant

T - Time-bound

You can use SMART goals for weight loss and fitness goals. It's about setting a goal, looking at it and breaking it down to becoming achievable in a certain amount of time.

Specific - I will lose weight in a certain amount of time or I will run five miles in a certain amount of time.

Measurable - Measurement is how you monitor your progress.

Achievable - Being realistic in your time frame to achieve your goals.

Relevant – Ensuring that what you are doing is entirely relevant to your weight loss or fitness goal.

Time-bound - Set a start date and a finishing date in which to achieve your goals.

Work out what your goals are and then sit down and write out a plan of action. Get a friend involved or do it by yourself. I've always found I work better on my own as if I start relying on someone else and they let me down for whatever reason it can be off putting. But everyone is different and you to need to find what works best for you. Ask yourself questions because only you know the answers.

How can I? What's the best way for me?

Lastly be kind to yourself. Enjoy the journey of self-discovery. Reward yourself. You could perhaps pay yourself for every workout or for every pound you lose, if money is a good incentive. Alternatively, have a cheat/ treat meal once a week IF you have been good and stuck to your healthy eating and exercise. But only if you have stuck to your plan for the whole week; if you have not, you must forego. Remember, this is a lifelong change, not a short term one. You will only get off your yo-yo diet merry go round if you get this embedded into your mind; Everything you do will either take you one step closer to your goal or one step further away. It's your choice. Become your own researcher in being a happier, healthier you.

One last tip before this chapter ends; most people tell themselves it's hard to lose weight. I hear this over and over again. I was also guilty of believing this before I started my own journey. So let's flip it.

It's EASY to drop weight when you do the right things, it really is. Because if you're doing the healthy eating and the exercise then how could it not be? Exercise and healthy eating become easier the more you do it. Smiley face. High five.

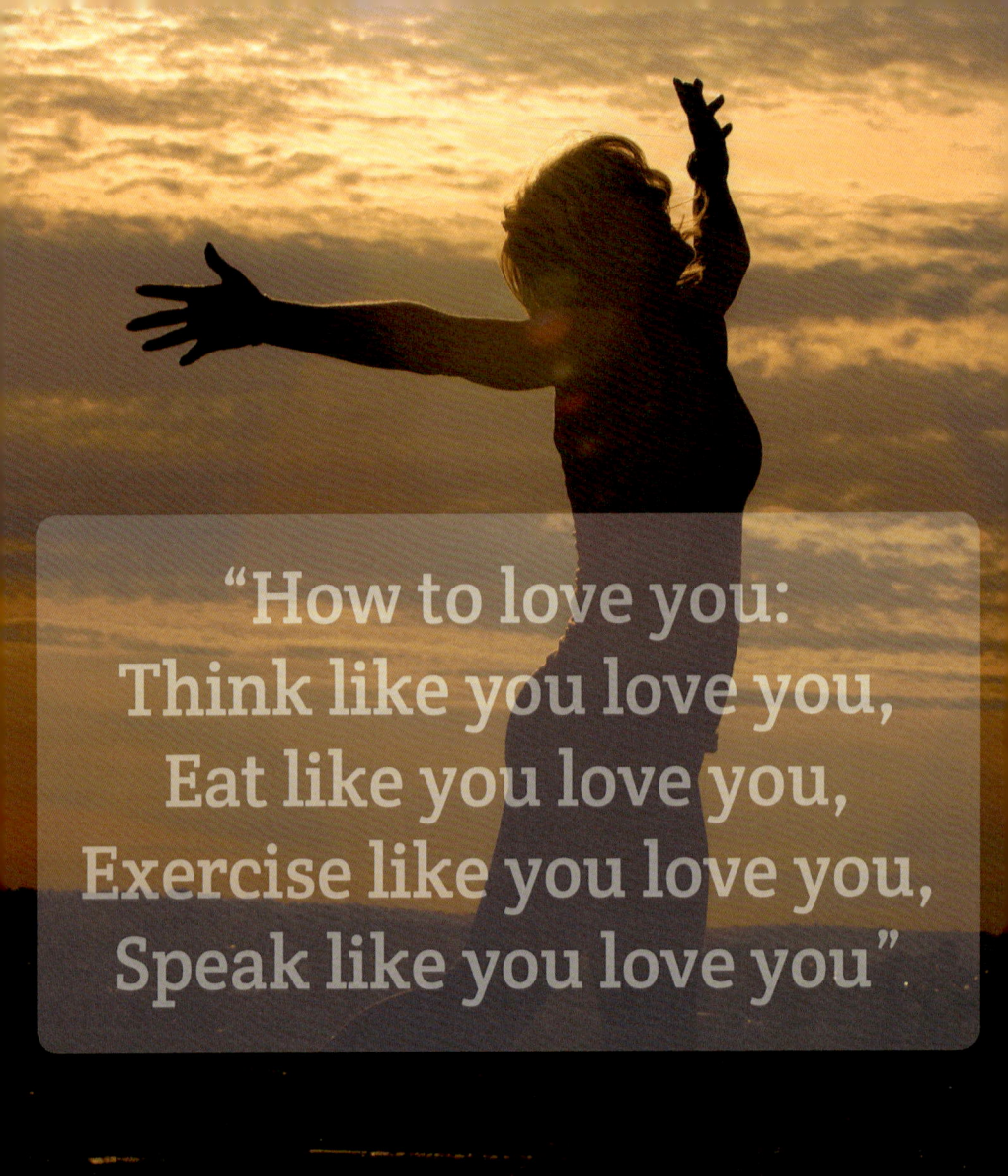

"How to love you:
Think like you love you,
Eat like you love you,
Exercise like you love you,
Speak like you love you"

6

Emotions

Emotions play a very important part of who we are. They make us feel, think and act in different ways. If we can master our emotions the same as our mind then the more self-control we will have over our bodies. Learning to love yourself is probably the number one emotion everyone should master, both male and female. The world would be a much nicer place if we all did. Loving yourself is not selfish, it's selfless. I didn't know how to love myself for many years. I hated myself. I hated being me. I thought that I wasn't good enough. I believed all the things I'd heard over the years. I believed that I'd never amount to much, being a teenage mother. I hardly had any qualifications to my name and I dropped out of school early so I did not take all of my exams.

As you know from my first chapter, I had a child in my teenage years and although my son Kieron is one of the best things to ever happen to me, he was also the making of me. In most people's eyes, even my own at that time, I wasn't destined for a very bright future. They were wrong. I was wrong. Your self-belief and your self-confidence comes about once you start loving yourself and taking care of yourself. It's all internal. Once you are in the right frame of mind, your feelings will follow suit. I started to look at myself in the mirror and slowly began loving myself exactly the way that I was. It was then that my body really started taking shape the way I wanted it to and this made me feel great. I discovered it was easier to change when I loved myself than it was when I hated myself.

What we resist persists; All the time I was hating myself into change, I didn't get anywhere fast. The moment I started loving myself into change everything fell into place and was so much easier. I had to accept myself the way I already was and know what I wanted in order for the change to take place. I forced myself to take a good long look in the mirror and start learning to love my body. My journey of self-love and acceptance started like that. I began by picking out the parts of me that I felt were good and asked myself what parts of me I loved. I loved my blue eyes. I loved my blonde hair (even if it isn't quite my natural colour ;)) I loved my smile. As I started looking down at my body, I realised I loved my boobs. Ha-ha, my beloved boobs again. I loved my ankles. That was about all I could master at first. Then slowly, I began to find other things I loved about myself. My freckles and belly button. My hands my nails, my toes, my feet, my knees; I do actually love my knees. I will kiss them in yoga when I come knee to face with them on occasions. Little by little, step by step, I began to find more things I loved about me; even my ears which I had once felt were enormous and would do anything and everything as a child to cover up.

The more I found to love, the easier it was and I soon found that I really did love all of me. I started to read up about self-love in order to educate myself about looking after not only my body but also my mind and emotions too; they are all very much connected and are really one and the same thing. Really incredible things start happening the moment you step into your own and you love being you. Making changes is so much easier when you already love the person you are.

So many people are living their life feeling sad or feeling bad about their past, somehow blaming themselves over and over for things that they cannot change. I read that if you're living your life in the past; you're depressed. And if you're thinking and worrying about the future you will suffer from anxiety and be anxious. Try to live in the here and now. Make the very best of every single day you have on this earth. Today is all we ever really have; tomorrow is not promised and yesterday is gone. Celebrate being you. You were given the gift of life. Make the very most of it. You were given a body to live in that is you. Be the very best version of you that you can be. I'm very thankful I'm me.

Everything I have been through has brought me to this day and made me the loving, happy person I am. My past hasn't made me bitter, it's made me better. Anything you have done in your past is a lesson, not a life sentence. Let go of anything from your past that doesn't serve you now. You can only ever learn from your past. Forgive yourself and move on. No matter what you have done or how many times you have failed in the past, it doesn't matter; every moment is a brand new fresh start. It's never too late for change. There's always a point. Wherever you are right now regardless of what time of the day or night it is, you really can choose to just start afresh. It's a choice. Your choice. Nobody can take that away from you. What you also find when you love being you is that nobody can compete with you as you are so happy in your own skin. You should NEVER measure yourself to someone else. If you do, you are doing yourself a terrible injustice. You are a unique individual.

YOU ARE BEAUTIFUL LIKF YOU AND I AM BEAUTIFUL LIKE ME. We need to stop comparing ourselves to others especially unrealistic, airbrushed pictures in magazines. If we used that time and energy to work on ourselves we wouldn't have the time or inclination to want to be anyone else but ourselves. Wc really are awesome; each and every one of us. When we truly love ourselves, we really don't care what anyone says or thinks about us, either.

What I've come to realise with time is that's their problem not ours. They have their own issues; their own limited self-belief. You're capable of amazing things. Don't let anyone ever talk you down or make you believe anything differently about yourself than what you already know. A friend once told me that as you get older, you get bigger. It happens to women of a certain age. I looked around me and saw women of all different sizes of all different ages and thought to myself no, not me. That's your limited belief not mine. Don't believe everything that is said to you. Some people think they know, but they do not. Only you know what's best for you. When you love yourself, you develop confidence and are so self-assured that no one's opinion but your own matters. It is water off a ducks back.

This brings me onto an emotion that is really holding some of us back. A lot of women are stuck or so busy looking at others when they could use that time and put that energy to better use by trying to be the best version of themselves they can be. If you were busy loving you, then this emotion really wouldn't come into it. I am, of course, talking about jealousy. I wish jealousy and envy did not exist as they are such negative emotions. They do far more harm than good. A new way to flip this emotion is to admire and aspire. If I see a woman who looks good, I will admire that woman. I may wonder what her secret is. I may even aspire to be like her in whatever way, knowing I will never be the same as her because she is her and I am me.

One of the things I've learnt to feel comfortable to do is give genuine compliments. I love telling someone how good they look. If someone catches my eye it's a pleasure for me to tell them something nice. It makes me feel good to make another feel good. Do good things as they will come back to you. Try it and see how it makes you feel. You cannot give a genuine compliment and not feel good about giving it. Being jealous of another person will get you nowhere fast, nor will being envious. If you're busy watering your own garden, you have no time to care what's going on in someone else's, because you are too busy taking care of your own. That's exactly how it should be.

Jealousy robs you of your happiness so do not entertain it. Drop the jealousy. If you feel it coming to the surface, recognise it. Take back your control and let it go. Nobody has time for that kind of negativity in their lives. I never think about being in competition with anybody else. The only person I compete with is myself. I only ever want to improve on being a better me. I'm a work in progress. I'm always learning, always working on me and evolving. Imagine what a beautiful world it would be if we were happy for each other and non-judgemental; if we all appreciated everyone's individuality for who they are. If you love yourself, all of this is possible. You reap what you sow. Give out what you most want back. How are you ever going to be happy if you're not happy for others? We must be happy for others to be happy ourselves; life is a reflection.

Happiness is an inside job; you have to choose to be happy. It's not external, it's internal. Work on your inside first and what's there will come through to the outside. I have met the most confident and happy women who are ordinary; not the most slim or most beautiful. They don't wear all the best clothes or carry designer handbags. They literally beam from the inside out and the confidence and happiness illuminates them in a way that makes them really attractive. It's shocking for me to see how females will tear each other down instead of building each other up. As women, regardless of age, race or religion we should stand shoulder to shoulder with each other. Strong, confident women support each other. They do not put each other down. That goes for men too.

You will rarely hear me say a bad word about myself. I remember the days that I would put myself down. I told myself I was fat, ugly and unattractive. I cringe when I think back to those days. How could I put myself down like that? Negative self-talk; that was then and this is now.

I once read an article that questioned how much money the beauty industry would lose if we all learned to love and accept ourselves just the way we are. It's definitely food for thought. You own your own feelings and emotions just as you are the creator of your own thoughts. Nobody else can make you happy; you must choose to be happy. Happiness is an inside job my beautiful friends. Know it is yours for the taking. If you can change your thoughts then you can definitely change the way you feel.

Exercise releases natural endorphins that help to make you happy. I know first-hand that this is true as I have overcome depression with exercise. I've managed the most stressful year of my life with exercise. I just wouldn't be the happy, confident person I am today without it. If you can find an exercise that you love to do, you will want to do it over and over again. I started out simply running and walking. Did you know that extra oxygen in the air is why walking or running outside clears your mind?

Not knowing what the outcome of my divorce would be for me and my children, used to leave me in terrible moods, so to conquer this, I would go for a walk or a run with my dogs in the fresh air. My mind would clear, my mood would lift and I would begin to feel happy again; I could see my direction more clearly. My mind would strengthen and I'd become convinced that I could handle this. That's how I coped each day. I never gave in and always found a way to manage as best I could. I managed my stress with exercise.

One night, just before my matrimonial court case, I was rushed to hospital in the middle of the night as I thought I was having a heart attack. I was told by the doctors that I had the heart of an athlete and was suffering from anxiety due to fearing my future. I knew that I had to just keep doing what I was doing. I had to stay positive for a positive outcome. I had to keep exercising to stay happy and clear headed. I had to keep taking one day at a time. It was like running the marathon; I just had to keep going to get to the end. Divorce, as horrible as it is, is a means to an end. I shared that with you because no matter what you go through in life you always have choices and ways of managing things. Keep making good choices and you will get a good outcome.

In life, I think we blame our bodies for our unhappiness, when all we need to do is change the way we do some things to look after ourselves better rather than beating ourselves up and pretending we have no self-control. This is something that's really good to know; when you cannot change your external, you have to change your internal and how you look at things. Life is 10% what happens to us and 90% of how we react to it. We have to decide as to how we will react to anything life throws at us. You always have a choice as to how you will react in return. Positively or negatively. If something is making you unhappy in your life, you have the power to change it. Be it your body, your job, your relationship or your life in general.

Once you start taking care of and loving yourself, then you start coming from a much more loving, caring place. Love and happiness are two of the most positive emotions we experience. Think about how happy you feel when you love something. It brings about good feelings of joy and pleasure.

It took a lot of practice for me to learn to love myself, but just as

I said the mind gets stronger, I believe that it's the same principle with your feelings too. You have to practice and get good at loving yourself and being happy. Studies have shown smiling with a pencil in between your teeth can give you a hit of real pleasure. Inducing a smile can change your mood, thus bringing about happiness even if you're not feeling particularly happy. You would think that you have to be happy first for a smile to come about, but actually it can be the other way around. If you force the smile then you will feel happy too. Smile first and the happiness will follow. The way this works is that your facial muscles send a message to your brain telling it you are smiling so the brain thinks you are happy, which in turn makes you feel happy. I smile a lot. I love smiling as it makes me feel so happy. Smiling costs nothing so it is such a simple pleasure. Smiling changes your mood and helps to relieve stress by releasing endorphins and serotonin. It works the same way as exercise does so you can't help but feel happy. The added bonus is that smiling makes you, without a doubt, more attractive. SMILE AT THE WORLD AND THE WORLD SMILES BACK.

It is a choice to be happy with yourself, and as we know from what we have already read, that choice comes from within. It's impossible to feel both happy and sad at the same time. Try it and see. Did you try? You cannot do it, can you? This shows that you can either choose to be happy or unhappy with your body. Given the choice, what would you rather be? I'd rather be happy with my body and make the right choices to ensure I find that happiness. If you love yourself, you cannot help but to be happy and love being you. Have a love affair with being you; you have to live with you for the rest of your life. Everything you think, feel, see, hear, all comes from within you. If you're happy with what God gave you and you make the very best of your body, it stands to reason it will serve you well.

When I didn't know where life would take me after my divorce, I didn't realise that I had everything I needed to have a happy and fulfilled life within me. All I ever needed was my body, my mind and my voice. In life you need nothing else to get on. Life is what you make it. The only time I experienced comfort eating in recent years is when I have a hangover and feel sorry for myself. I tend not to be able to eat anything because I feel too ill to eat. I know comfort eating and eating disorders are a big problem for some people and I feel for you. If you suffer from emotional eating of any kind, please for your own sake, open up; speak to someone, a friend or family member or your doctor for help and guidance. NHS Choices has some good advice on their website www.nhs.uk Do not suffer in silence as many do. Get help.

To keep your mind in check, you have to tell yourself that you have lots of self-discipline, willpower and determination. Because it's going to get you to where you want to be and the body you want. You are going to come face to face with lots of different circumstances, and your self-discipline is going to need to kick in if you are going to succeed in your fitness and weight loss goals. You're going to need to learn to say no to lots of different things. It goes back to asking yourself this one question; is whatever it is going to get me to where I want to be? If the answer is yes, do it and if the answer is no, be strong and say no.

I've been really fortunate that I have managed to get myself to where I wanted to be mostly without any outside medical help. I didn't go to the doctors to go on anti-depressants but I do know lots of people that do go on them for one reason or another, and that's your personal choice. For me, I wanted to see if the natural remedy of exercise would work, and I'm so very pleased that it did.

There are lots of homeopathic/alternative medicines out there that also help with lots of issues with mind and emotional blocks for weight loss. Look into all of your different options as that's the only way you can ever make an informed decision that is the right choice for you.

We now have our minds and emotions in the right place.

It is time to move onto nutrition.

7

Nutrition

Fitness is 80% what we eat and 20% exercise. What you are putting into your body is and should be paramount to exercise. Not the other way around. I'd like to point out that I eat more food now than what I used to eat in the past. It's just I eat more of the good food and less of the bad food. I love food; I love the enjoyment of choosing food. I most definitely love eating it. I have a sweet tooth that is pretty much under control.

I remember well the days of starving myself to lose weight. It may have even worked for you like it did for me, initially. It's just not sustainable. If you have ever tried this method, it not only makes you irritable and miserable, your body goes into what's known as starvation mode which means it holds onto your fat even more, because it doesn't know when you're going to eat again. This, in turn makes it even harder for you to drop weight. Your body is clever like that. Starving yourself and short term dieting doesn't work. Eating a healthy diet long term, nourishing your body and exercising does. Would you really want to be on that short term weight loss diet for the rest of your life? The moment you hit your target weight and revert back to your old eating habits, you will put the weight you lost back on and probably gain even more. I hear it and I see it and that was once me before I got it.

I do not keep the bad foods in my house that I know I couldn't eat responsibly. Cakes, sweets, crisps, chocolate, biscuits and basically anything that's not good for me are things that I won't keep in my home. I only eat these things as a treat and have to physically leave my house to go and buy it. I only buy what I want and no more. It's a simple method and it works. I have been in maintenance mode for over ten years and have managed to stay the same healthy weight.

I have found what works for me is five days of fairly strict healthy eating and two days off. The weekends are my time out. I really look forward to the weekend where I eat and drink whatever I want, within reason. As soon as Monday comes around again, I'm back on my healthy eating track.

I'm not a massive drinker thankfully; Not at home anyway. I'd rather eat my calories than drink them. I prefer not having hangovers. I love waking up with a clear head and mind. What I know about alcohol is it's a stimulant and a depressant, people will drink it to help them unwind and relax and to help send them to sleep, but because it's a stimulant it does not help you to have the best night's sleep. Alcohol mostly gives you negative thoughts and feelings which is why it is considered a depressant. Monitor how you feel the day after you have been drinking alcohol. I find I no longer care about eating healthily and will be in a negative mind-set. I feel down and this may only last a day or two, but that's a day or two too long in my book. If you genuinely want to be happy with your body, alcohol is not the answer.

I want to be at my best during the working week while I am spending time with my clients; I want to perform to the best of my ability and alcohol just doesn't fit into my healthy midweek regime. I save it for the weekend, but to be honest, it's not a big part of my life now. I may have a drink once a month but since I found out that the toxins in alcohol act as poison within my body, I tend to be sick. My body cannot cope with the alcohol. The healthier you are, the less tolerance your body will have towards alcohol. Alcohol will hinder you if you want to lose weight or reach your full potential in fitness. If you're serious about losing weight and getting healthy, cut it out until you hit your goals, then reintroduce it back in slowly. Just like me, you might find that you don't even miss it. I gave up alcohol for four months during my bikini fitness training, and I had said to myself that drinking alcohol was going to take me further from my goal rather than closer to it, so not drinking alcohol was an easy choice to make.

One drink that will take you towards your goal again and again and will absolutely help you to get the body you want, is the beautiful H2O otherwise known as water. I hear time and time again that people don't like drinking water and I really get it because I didn't used to like drinking it either. Guess what I was saying to myself? Answers on a postcard ha-ha. I don't like drinking water so I didn't drink it. But then I flipped it. Now I love drinking water because it's so good for me. It wasn't until I read up about the benefits of drinking water and how good it is, that I started to drink it. Water is not only good for your body; it is also good for your brain function and your skin too. Once I got this into my head, I knew that to have a healthy body one must drink water and that's when I accepted that it had to be a big part of my lifelong healthy regime. Guidelines state that we should be drinking 2 to 3 litres per day; this is around eight medium size glasses of water. I tell my clients that it's one of their number one weight loss tools. I literally start drinking water the moment my eyes open in the morning. People often complain that drinking a lot of water makes you wee more. This is certainly true, as what goes in must come out.

My advice to you would be to drink two glasses of water as soon as you wake up in the morning. I go for 1 litre first thing. Try taking it up to bed so it's there as soon as you wake or leave it out on the side so it's the first thing you do when you come down for breakfast in the morning. It's best to drink the water first thing as it then has time to get through you before you leave the house. Water takes approximately one hour to go through your body. Most people give themselves an hour and half to get ready and get out the house in the morning so most of the water should have made its way out of you before you leave the house for the school run or work. Just make sure you have your timings right so you don't get caught short. I think I know where every public toilet is within a ten mile radius of my home, funnily enough.

The benefits of drinking water first thing in the morning on an empty stomach are:

- It flushes your bowels

- It prevents constipation

- It helps flush out toxins

- It kick starts your metabolism

- It helps you to lose weight

- It helps you to maintain weight

- It boosts your immunity

- It helps prevent headaches

- It is good for your skin

- It quenches your thirst

- It has zero calories

Water is now my favourite drink. I love drinking it. We wouldn't be alive for long without it. I will sometimes go crazy and have sparkling if I'm out in a restaurant or bar, but mostly I'm happy to drink filtered tap water. How could you not like it with all those amazing benefits? If you struggle with drinking eight glasses a day, start with just one and build on that. Set yourself a SMART goal and make it happen to get to eight glasses of water in a certain amount of time. You'll find you're so busy trying to fit drinking that amount of water into your day that you really won't be thinking so much about food.

If you really want to do something, be it drinking water or eating healthy food, then set yourself a goal and make it a challenge. There is nothing more self-satisfying than achieving your goals. I get so proud and congratulate myself when I achieve things. Like drinking my target of water intake for the day. I'm like well done to me. Make drinking the right amount of water a challenge. It will become a habit in no time. Trust me. You'll then wonder how you ever lived any differently. We water plants to ensure they don't die so we need to keep our bodies topped up as they are made up mostly of water. The colour of your wee is a great indicator of whether or not you are drinking enough water. It should be a light yellow straw colour or champagne if that makes you smile. Darker yellow means you may be dehydrated but it's really important for wellness and optimal good health to drink lots of water. Seriously, learn to love it. Water is your friend. Best drinking partner ever.

You will be more successful with healthy eating and drinking water if you plan ahead. You'll stay on track effortlessly. You will not go hungry because you'll have planned your food in advance. I write down my weekly meal plan each Sunday night for the following week.

If you are not drinking enough, your body will recognise being hungry when in fact it is actually thirsty, so always drink a glass of water first when hunger pangs hit. Being hungry is your body's way of telling you that you're running low on fuel. I eat three healthy meals a day and if I need a snack then it's a healthy snack like a small handful of nuts, a spoonful of peanut butter or some dried fruit. I will have this with me so I do not get tempted to buy or eat the wrong stuff if I'm out. Peanut butter comes in sachets now, would you believe?

I start every day with breakfast. Most people have their evening meal by 8pm at the latest and then we sleep, so it stands to reason that you are going to need to refuel when you wake up 10-12 hours after you last ate. Your brain is the first organ that's affected if your food supply is depleted. Without breakfast, you will not be at your best for the day and it will be difficult for you to think straight. You are also more likely to eat all of the wrong things for the rest of the day as you will be hungry. I used to think skipping breakfast was the answer, thinking that eating two meals was better than three to keep the weight off, but it is not, for the reasons that I've stated. Eating breakfast is very important for weight loss and management and it is something I have done every day for the past eleven or so years. I'm starving come breakfast time.

Have you ever gone food shopping when you are hungry? What do you end up buying? You buy all of the wrong things because you just want to eat anything and everything. I am giving you the best advice ever; don't go food shopping when you're hungry.

I start the day with the healthiest drink which is water then I fuel my body with good food. I will eat a high carbohydrate breakfast. I also have a banana every morning. Did you know that bananas can make you happy as they have high levels of tryptophan that is converted into serotonin which is known as the happy hormone?

Food affects your mood, it really does.

We all know deep down how to eat healthily. For me, food is my fuel. It not only keeps me alive, it also helps me to run efficiently. One way of thinking about it is to compare your body to that of a car. If I don't put petrol in, I'm going nowhere fast. Now if I want to run like a Rolls Royce or a sports car I need to fill myself up with optimal fuel. I need to be thinking about what kind of fuel my body needs to nourish it. Nourishing yourself prevents you from getting ill and keeps you healthy, and fuel helps to run you. You need both.

Fruit and vegetables are on the top of my list for optimal fuel. I know from the fairly small amount of nutrition information that I covered whilst doing my PT course that carbohydrates are our preferred source of food that we convert into energy/fuel the most efficiently. Sixty percent carbohydrates, twenty five percent protein and fifteen percent good fats is the percentage that I aim for. As a result, my breakfast will usually be, either porridge with some dried fruit or brown seeded toast with peanut butter (crunchy, no sugar added) and a banana. I have recently gone vegetarian and I love it. I only eat the foods that I love so eating healthily is a joy to me. I cannot tell you how excited I get at the thought of breakfast in the morning. It really is the simple pleasures in life that make you so happy to be alive.

I will have a green tea first thing in the morning because it's a good hot drink to have. I know if I start my day healthily, I make healthy choices throughout the rest of the day. I only have one cup of coffee a day and I will have that mid-morning as I want a caffeine kick as a boost to push me through to lunch. I like it black and strong. Double espresso BOOM. Once upon a time it was a latte, but I went from that to cappuccino then macchiato to now no milk at all. (If you're trying to give something up doing it in stages works a treat.) When you're exercising, you want as little fluid sloshing around in your stomach as possible so coffee is a great pre workout drink as it's known to enhance your training performance. Remember to drink water to hydrate as you work out. I've been told recently about having a beetroot juice shot. Apparently it gives a good energy boost without the caffeine, so if you're caffeine free or you want to give up caffeine then this could be a good alternative and one of your 5 a day.

I have my fruit in the morning then once lunchtime comes, I change to vegetables. I love salads for lunch with some form of carbohydrate because I need fuel for the afternoon. What I had for breakfast will determine what I have for lunch. The last meal of my day is dinner, where I go for more protein and vegetables with a small amount of carbs like a sweet potato, depending on how hungry I am or if I'm going out to work or exercise. You can eat a lot of vegetables to fill you up, as long as they are not too much root vegetables. Eating meals in this way is how I now eat more food than I have ever done before. I just eat more of the good stuff and less of the bad. It really is as simple as that. I read you should eat like a king for breakfast, a prince for lunch and a pauper at dinner, I like this theory and it works for me. I stay away from white food like white bread, white potatoes, white rice, white pasta and white sugar. I try to stick to foods that are brown or wholemeal. I mostly have sugar if it's naturally occurring in fruits and food. Sugar is really bad for you and highly addictive. I rarely eat processed food or takeaways and I always have a camomile tea to go to bed with as it aids sleep.

I used to have a massive addiction to chocolate but I now mostly eat seventy or eighty five percent dark chocolate because it's quite bitter and you only want to eat a little bit of it at a time. Any chocolate that is seventy percent cocoa content or more, is actually quite good for you in moderation. I also eat dried fruits which helps to keep my sweet tooth under control. When you're not eating or having sugar in tea or coffee, anything you eat that's naturally sweet will then taste much sweeter. You really don't need to eat that much of it then to satisfy your sweet tooth.

If I know I am going to be out for the day and may struggle to find healthy food, I make my own in advance and take it with me in my bag. It was whilst taking part in the bikini fitness contest that I really learned how to plan ahead with food. I always kept my food in plastic containers with an ice pack to be sure I could eat the right foods at the right time. I don't rely on anyone but me for my food intake. There are not many things we can control in our lives, but what we put into our bodies is one thing we can. We must look after and cherish our body because it is the only one we have.

I find if I eat crap food I feel crap. I am so used to eating healthily now that when I relax on holiday and eat what I want, I find that after a few days I don't feel good because of the food and drink that I have consumed. I think my body is so finely tuned now that eating junk food makes me feel sick and lethargic. I actually find myself looking forward to getting back to my normal, healthy routine. The best way to describe it is that I eat clean. The largest part of my diet is fruit and vegetables, followed by carbohydrates, protein and then good fats. I also eat a spoonful of coconut oil every day. I personally feel I have a really good balanced diet.

Before I became a vegetarian, I did a lot of research to make sure that I'd still be getting all the right foods and nourishment that my body needs. I have to find other foods that contain protein as I'm no longer getting that from animal source.

My favourite foods as a vegetarian are;

- Porridge oats and bran
- Quinoa
- Chick peas
- Pulses and lentils
- Avocado
- Green leafy vegetables such as spinach, kale and various salad leaves
- Sweet Potato
- Peanut butter
- Bananas
- Berries, like strawberries, blueberries and raspberries
- Citrus fruits

I cook with olive oil and coconut oil and put a spoonful of coconut oil in with my porridge whenever I have it. I love the taste of coconut.

I'd like to talk about coconut oil at this point. It's magic in a pot. I only wish I'd found it sooner; Google reasons for eating coconut oil! It nourishes you from the inside out. We must have healthy fats as part of our diet in order for our nails, hair, brain and skin function as they should. It also aids with weight loss and weight management; the list goes on. On top of all this, it saves me a lot of money on body moisturiser as I smother myself in it after a shower or bath. Just make sure you wear cotton pyjamas so as not to ruin your bed sheets. The oil will soak into your skin during the night and in the morning your skin will be soft and glowing. This is my number one beauty product as it will keep my skin looking so much younger for longer. Experts say that our skin absorbs anything we put onto it but coconut oil is natural so it can only be good for us, and will not make us ill like other products could. Be beauty product smart. You can even brush your teeth with it, and take your makeup off with it. As you can probably tell, I love coconut oil and only buy organic virgin cold pressed, which most supermarkets stock now.

I spend a lot of time on the NHS Choices website and would encourage you to do so too. There is an Eatwell plate as well lots of up to date health related topics, all in one place. And because it's NHS, it should also be consistent with what a doctor would tell you if you had to go and see them for health advice. If I was worried about what I was eating or I really needed help to come up with a balanced healthy diet, I would spend money and go to see a nutritionist. There are so many food related allergies out there now it's best to see a specialist who really knows about these things as a doctor may not go into any great depth with dietary advice.

I know I should be eating carbohydrates in the morning and in the early part of the afternoon because I will have more time to burn them off but what you do not use as fuel when eating carbohydrate will be stored in the body as fat. It's best then for your evening meal to be more protein with lots of vegetables to fill you up.

When I had to lose a stone in weight in six weeks before my bikini fitness contest the eating plan I was given for the first few weeks allowed me to have carbs for breakfast but for the rest of the day it was all green vegetables and lean protein. In the last two weeks, I had no carbs and all as I just stuck to protein. I had a very restricted eating plan. I ate little and often throughout the day whilst drinking water. I dropped weight easily.

It's important to have a meal plan that works for you, because I cannot bear to be hungry. The new word for it is 'hangry.' There is an eating plan for clients of Happy You, Happy Body Bootcamp, and I am confident that it is a plan that works. You can purchase this eating plan online at blurb www.blurb.co.uk/b/6450481-f42-fat-shredding-feast-diet-plan. I started with this plan for the first few months of my contest and when I had to lose a few pounds after the Christmas period. This plan should ensure that you never go hungry which suits me down to the ground. I never want to go hungry. I'm happy when fed and I've eaten adequately. I spent years doing it wrong and felt elated when I realised that all I had to do was eat healthily and drink water. It felt like I had discovered a secret that I had chosen to ignore all along. It was so obvious! There is no magic pill or quick fix diet that will get you long term results.

When you exercise and workout, the last thing you want to do is eat anything that's going to jeopardise all of your hard work. Working out does not mean you can go on to eat anything you want. If you eat crap, you will not get the healthy body you desire and you will undo all your hard work. Why would you do that? Eating healthily, drinking water and exercising is the healthy balance to looking and feeling great and having a great relationship with your body.

You really do need to put time into doing your own research as we are all unique and what works for one person may not work for another. You have to understand what you're putting into your body, and it's nobody else's responsibility but your own. Rely on no one but you. My rule of thumb is to read the ingredients on the back of the foods I buy. If I cannot understand or pronounce the words I won't buy it. No additives, no food enhancers, no preservatives. Buy fresh and eat clean. I feel most passionate about this.

They say most cancers and heart disease are preventable and I think it seems fairly obvious that a lot of illnesses are coming from what we are putting into our bodies. The advice was always that we eat five portions of fruit or veg a day to stay healthy, but they have recently increased that to ten. I want to be healthy and stay healthy. What I eat and drink now makes the biggest difference to all of this. It stands to reason then that I must make good healthy choices right now to provide me with a good, healthy body now and for my future years.

For the past eleven or so years my body has looked how I want it to look. I am feeling how I want to feel. I am happy, healthy, fit and active. If I want to stay this way then I must continue this way. I trust that I understand what I am putting into my body so you must also take control over what goes into yours. Let food be your fuel and exercise be your stress release. Eat yourself happy and healthy. Make food and water your friends, not your enemy.

You'll either find a way or you'll find an excuse the choice is yours.

"YOU are BEST project YOU will EVER work on"

8
Training

There are many different styles of training to keep fit. I believe if you find a training technique that you love you will want to keep doing it over and over again, just as I have. It took time to figure out what exercises I really enjoyed doing and you will have to find what ones you enjoy doing too.

You could ask yourself these types of questions;

- What would I love to do to keep fit?

- What exercise regime will fit into my life the easiest?

- What can I afford to do? (As most classes and gym memberships cost money.)

Here are many different types of training to consider;

- **Running** - Teach yourself - join a Running Group

- **Walking** - Power walking - Brisk walking - Hiking

- **Water Sports** - Swimming - Water aerobics - Surfing

- **Dancing** - Zumba - Salsa -Boogie Bounce

- **Martial Arts** - Judo -Karate -Self Defence

- **Gym** - Join in classes - Use gym equipment

- **Home train** - Workout DVD's - YouTube

- **Cycling** - Mountain bike off road - on road

- **Ball sports** - Football - Rugby -Golf - Bowls

- **Racket sports** - Tennis - Badminton - Squash

- **Other** – Bootcamp - Yoga - Pilates

The list goes on. Look up fitness in your local area on google or look in the local paper. You are your best investment as far as money and time are concerned. Your health is your greatest wealth. I'm not sure how many years you think you have in you, but for me, I don't see why there is any reason I cannot remain healthy into my early nineties, as my grandma's have all lived long lives and if I want to remain healthy and active, I have to invest in me now.

When I took up running in my late thirties, the reason I chose not to join a gym was that I didn't have the time. I had to find something that was time effective and fit in to my already busy life. Once you factored in travelling time, gym gear and booking the crèche, it would take a whole morning to fit in an hours' worth of exercise. It just didn't make any sense.

I have been running and power walking now for over a decade and I love it. All I need to do is put my comfortable workout gear and trainers on and then I am off. It is easy. If you want to improve your workout, you can power walk and wear ankle weights or carry hand weights. I will do an upper body workout as I walk along a very busy main road. I have noticed there are more men power walking now and it's great to see. Power walking is not just for women.

Sometimes people wave or beep their horns at me and I smile back when I can. People love people who try. I'm doing something to keep fit and I really don't mind if people stare at me. Someone once shouted out of the window at me. Luckily I laughed at the *"go on fatty!"* but I can see how this might discourage someone from exercising outside in a public place. My advice is to ignore it. You're doing something for yourself. It's their problem, not yours and when people say negative things, it's a reflection of how they feel about themselves and really has nothing to do with you. Keep doing what you're doing, regardless.

As a single parent, money was often an issue but running or power walking costs nothing except the price of a decent pair of trainers and a sports bra.

I know when you have young children it is not easy to get any time for yourself but you must try to make some time to look after you. This will then enable you to look after your little ones to the best of your ability. Go for a brisk walk with your buggy or purchase one that you can run with. Take turns with your partner to look after the children so that one of you can go out to exercise. Workout DVD's or fitness channels on YouTube are also great ways for busy mums to find time to work out as you can download them on to a smart phone, tablet or laptop. Always start with the beginners' version and work up to harder, more advanced exercises. Do a bit of research on the internet to find one that you like the sound of when your children are sleeping or watching television. Stick it on and do it. There's nothing stopping your children from joining in. My daughters have come power walking with me and have done the workout DVD's with me at home for as long as I can remember. I love them joining in with me, and I'm leading by example so that my daughters will follow suit.

The benefits of taking up regular exercise are endless. It lowers the risk of many chronic illnesses such as heart disease, Type 2 diabetes, and lessens your chances of suffering from a stroke or developing some cancers. Exercise boosts self-esteem, lifts your mood and improves sleep quality. It gives you energy and reduces your risk of depression, dementia and Alzheimer's disease. Dr Nick Cavill, a health promotional assistant says that if exercise was a pill, it would be one of the most cost- effective drugs ever invented.

I really do believe that exercise should be an integral part of everyone's lives. It's essential to help you lead an active, healthy, happy, long life. An excuse I often hear from people is that they don't have time for exercise, but if you cut down the amount of time you watched TV in the evenings, I'm sure you would have an hour in which to workout. I understand that watching television helps you to unwind and relax, but it's not making you healthy is it? Not unless you have a workout DVD on and you're moving your body in front of it. That could work. Just for an hour.

There's nothing to stop you working out with your partner. They say that the couples that train together stay together as you have a common interest of being healthy as a couple; it is such a good joint interest to have. And even if your partner is reluctant at first, once they see the changes in you, it won't be long before they want to join in! Stick to it and go it alone if you have to though. As the saying goes, you can bring a horse to water but you cannot make it drink. That's why I make a point of only helping those that are ready to change with my support, help and guidance. In order for change to happen, you have to want it to happen. Otherwise, we are both wasting our time.

The best thing I ever did exercise wise was teach myself to run. Running is one of the best ways to drop weight as you burn the most calories when you run. It is also great for cardio strength and stamina, depending on how fast you run. Power walking is a good second. If you're particularly heavy I recommend you power walk until you're a little lighter. Think about your joints. You want them to go on for a very long time and grass running is better for your joints than road running. Training for the marathon meant I had to run at the weekends and early in the morning before my family woke. I would run up and down country lanes on my own from around 6am every morning during the lighter months. I loved doing this as it was so peaceful just listening to the birds singing when no one else was around. The roads at that time in the morning were clear so I just had the trees and fields for company.

If you cannot run due to injuries, then walk. Many people are told they cannot run due to medical reasons but that does not stop them from walking. I was advised by a specialist that I couldn't run any more due to my back pain. This was just after I qualified as a personal trainer and I was devastated to hear that as my new career was based on my ability to run. After some thought, the specialist advised that I would have to learn to run on the balls of my feet like a llama because it takes the pressure off of your lower back as your heel is no longer hitting the floor first. I adapted my run to suit this and have now seen many other people adopting this same technique. To be honest, this discovery led to good things as I learned to power walk and then moved on to power yoga once I started training for the bikini fitness contest. Power yoga has been amazing for my back and posture, and due to this I no longer suffer from back pain and for three years have not had to have a pain relief injection. I will talk more about yoga further on in the book. Running heel to toe is the only way I run now apart from when I do hill sprint training when I have to revert back to running on the balls of my feet.

I've tried lots of different styles of training over the years and I advise you to give lots of things a go. I tell my clients to do what is best for them, whether it is at the gym or in their own home. I trained mostly in my own home to prove that you do not need to go to a gym to get a bikini fit body. You don't even have to go out for cardio training if you don't want to as you can use your stairs. Try running up and down them or going up them two at a time. If you don't have access to stairs then jog on the spot. If dancing takes your fancy, then do that; just be sure to warm up before you exercise and stretch out at the end of a workout.

I know a lot of people do not like to work out in a gym environment for whatever reason. You don't have to. With very little equipment it can all be done in the comfort of your own home. It really is down to personal choice. There are many big advantages to working out at home. There is no travel time, no gym membership and you don't require any childcare. Work out in your back garden if you have one! My home backs onto a park which is where I go to work out. On occasion, I have taken my boot camp inductees and clients to work out there as it is an ideal space. I personally love being out in the fresh air to workout, which is why I loved bootcamp training as soon as I discovered it. I didn't think I would like getting muddy and dirty but I really do. I'm at one with nature when I'm out in all weathers and it makes me feel the most alive. It's fun working out with other people too. When people are fitness minded they seem to be driven and focused. We all encourage each other. The only competition is with you. It's great for me to take part in the bootcamp as well as teach it because I get to see what it's like from both sides of the fence and I really believe it makes me a better trainer.

A few years ago, I discovered yoga and it is another way of training that I love and will do for the rest of my life. I was under the impression that it was a slow, boring exercise designed for older people but I couldn't have been more wrong. There are many different styles of yoga but I recommend you start with a beginner's class if you have the option, especially if you have never done yoga before. Yoga keeps you younger for longer; it conditions your muscles, keeps you supple and makes you flexible. It helps to keep your body and mind strong. Try it and see! Setting yourself a goal in training is a sure way to keep on track especially if you have a tendency not to see things through. I've trained a number of clients now to run, one of my Mad Mothers Bootcamp mums ran her first marathon recently. If I hadn't signed up for running the London Marathon I am sure my life would be very different now. I should have tried a 5 kilometre race first, and then run a 10k to build up to a half marathon, then a full marathon, but I threw myself in at the deep end which is just like me. But then who's to say it was wrong?

This is a good place for me to tell you more about how running the marathon had such a profound effect on me; I was around the three quarter mark of the marathon when my negative self-talk kicked in. I was watching much younger people than I was running passed me and I started to wonder why I'd done this at all. I started to think I was too old to be running the marathon. I was mad to think I could do this. At this stage, the negativity nearly beat me as I considered giving up. Thank God for Madonna and my iPod. There's a song on her Confessions on the dance floor album called 'Hung Up' and that song got me through. I can hear that song in my head right now.... *"Time goes by so slowly;"* It sure does around the three quarter mark of running a marathon. I eventually crossed the finish line. I remember what went through my mind, as clear as day; thank f*** for that. Even though I was completely exhausted I congratulated the woman to the right of me and we stopped and had a chat and she told me that it was her eighteenth marathon. This lady was in her seventies. Right then I stopped feeling miserable and started to feel happy and elated that I had completed a marathon. If this woman who was nearly double my age could do that, then so could l! Not to mention that she finished at the same time as I did. That was my biggest life lesson. You're never too old and if you don't use it, you will lose it. If you have it, keep going so that you'll always have it. I am now in a great frame of mind when it comes to my age as it has worked for me rather than against me whilst pursuing my career. Women like the fact I am older and that I have had children as I understand what they are going through. Plus, I don't look my age.

My solicitors once asked me about the working life span of a personal trainer and I was able to tell them, with confidence that it would last a very long time.

I have now learnt that exercise keeps me young. I cannot tell you how thankful I am for that lesson. What an amazing woman that lady was. I'm eternally grateful to her. She has no idea of what a positive effect she has had on me. Awesome woman.

After I had a second Caesarean section, I was told by the doctors that I would never again have a flat stomach, but I was determined to prove them wrong. I knew I didn't want to go down the surgery route, as some of the women I have come across that have had surgery have not been entirely happy with their end results. In fact the majority of women that I know that have had cosmetic surgery be it liposuction, breast implants or tummy tucks have more or less said to me they were disappointed or didn't realise that somewhere down the line they had created another problem. The problems range from scars to the fat from liposuction relocating elsewhere on the body, to infections. Or, the woman finds she is still not happy with her body even if the surgery was entirely successful, and goes on to want surgery to change something else. I have had three children, and when I look at my body I know it is not perfect but

I feel it is still perfect for me. The stretch marks and scars are all part of me, as without them I wouldn't have my children, and I have accepted that. I wouldn't want it any other way because for every woman wishing they didn't have them there's a woman wishing that she did. That alone should tell you just how lucky you are to have yours. I see young and old alike now with stretch marks and cellulite. It's nothing to be ashamed of, it is what it is. Be perfect in your imperfections; that is what beauty is.

At the end of the day if you want to go down the cosmetic surgery route it's your choice. Do your research; know the pros and cons and consider the future and how will it look as you grow older so you can make an informed decision. I personally would rather make the best of what I've got. Exercise has helped me to make the best of what I've got and my body is more than good enough for me. It's as good as it can be.

This brings me on to the face. I have done facial exercises for around ten years now, ever since I really got into running. I wake up every morning and I do ten minutes of facial exercises either before or after breakfast, depending on if I can wait that long to eat. I sit crossed legged in front of my mirror and I do around ten exercises for my face and neck. The human face has fifty seven muscles in it. I had heard that running, especially pavement running, is particularly hard on the face. Pounding those pavements can cause you to age quicker. I was already feeling old in my thirties; I didn't need to look old too. I thought about what I could do to stop this from happening. I discovered a book called 'The New Facercise' by Carole Maggio and it has become my face bible. I have now been using what I learned in this book for over a decade. I get many compliments that I don't look my age and as you can imagine I'm very happy about that and I know it's down to not only exercising my body and my face, but also eating healthily and taking care of my mind and emotions; it's the whole caboodle.

As we get older our muscles diminish (they shrink basically) but if you work out your facial muscles just like your body muscles through exercising them, the skin doesn't sag as the muscles shrink and your skin stays plump and young looking. I started noticing I was getting sagging skin and signs of a double chin in my late thirties, but because of this book, I no longer worry about it. I highly recommend reading it. The exercises are easy enough to do with easy to follow directions. People are always asking for demonstrations! It's hilarious. There are some really funny faces being pulled. All I know is that I am living proof that it works. I'm sure I will continue to do them for the rest of my life. No thank you Botox you're not for me.

Once you see and feel the results from physical training, you will wonder how you ever got along without it. Although I used to loathe exercise, once I could see the benefits, I never again wanted my life to be any other way. I actually feel bad if I don't work out now. I schedule exercise into my life and I just do it.

You'll probably think me mad but I imagine myself as a hamster on a hamster wheel going continually round. That's me with my exercise and healthy eating. I get off and have a break on weekends and special occasions like my birthday, holidays, Christmas and Easter but I get straight back on it again once I'm done with the time out. Although I cannot wait to get back to my healthy lifestyle, it is important to relax a little and enjoy life. Life is for living, after all. Just get straight back on that wheel once you're done with your time out.

I have joined a gym again recently after having trained at home for many years. I wanted a change and found a local gym that was in walking distance from my home. It means I have a choice to walk, run or drive there. It's been a change for me to work out in a gym environment. It's a family run gym, really personal and the owner Lee Chapman knows everyone's name. I love that. Great banter in there. If you can afford it, get yourself a personal trainer to show you what to do. They will create a personalised training regime just for you and show you how to use all the machines correctly, with good form to prevent injuries. They will also motivate you and push you that little bit harder. They get the best out of you for the best results. For people who have no idea how to use a gym, a personal trainer is ideal and will put you on the right track to getting your fitness to where you want it to be. If you make it clear to your trainer what it is you're looking for then they will work around you and your budget. It's definitely worth investing in.

It's the same for home fitness training. Getting a personal trainer to come to your home means they will bring equipment and show you the best places to workout in your home. Not much area or equipment is needed for this. Your own body weight can give you a great workout. If I go on holiday and there's no gym where I'm staying I just do some body weight exercises to keep up my fitness. If I'm lying down all day by the pool then one hour of exercise before doing this is going to make me feel I have earned my rest.

Rest is where this chapter will end nicely. Rest and a peaceful night's sleep is one of the best outcomes of being active; it's the added bonus of exercise. I sleep so well. Muscles repair whilst we sleep. Sleeping is so underrated. If you're rundown or tired, not getting enough sleep will play havoc on your healthy eating and your training. It will also be harder for you to stay focused. I adore my sleep. For me it's seven to eight hours every night. Working out, eating healthily, drinking water and sleeping well is how I make sure

I have a good quality of life. It's having this equilibrium in your life that makes you feel happy and content. It's nice to feel that all's well in your world.

It was at this point in my book that I had a change of heart and decided to change the name of my book and my Bootcamp Company; Mad Mothers Mission wasn't sitting right. After some thought, I decided I wanted the book to be called Happy You, Happy Body. My Bootcamp Company will be the Happy You, Happy Body Bootcamp. I want to be known as the happy body creator. This feels really right for me. It is me and how I want to be known. It better illustrates the message I am trying to convey when I talk about my life and my book. It is about happy bodies and learning to love yourself.

"Put your workout gear on. Make your workout happen"

9

Attire

So, back to my book. Where was I? Yes, attire.

mantra for slimming is health over weight loss and for clothing it is comfort over brand. I live in my active wear five days a week. It's my work uniform if you like. I am really happy that I get to work in my comfortable workout clothes. I feel like I'm always ready for exercise and if I then want to choose to workout myself between clients or Bootcamps then I can. Which is just great for me. Wearing the right workout attire will also put you into the right fitness mind-set.

If you struggle to fit exercise into your life as a busy mum then putting on your active wear first thing in the morning means you're ready to work out as and when you get a moment to yourself to do it. You could wear your active wear to work if you walk, run or bike it to get there and back. That is a great way to schedule in exercise. Just arrive a little earlier to freshen up and take your work clothes with you. Taking your active wear to work to hit the gym en-route home is another great idea too. I keep a spare change of fitness clothes in my car just in case I get rained on or very sweaty whilst working or training. Baby wipes are also a godsend for those days when I get particularly smelly.

Being a bootcamp instructor and taking part in bootcamp means I train outside in the rain and muddy fields, as a result, there's no point in wearing expensive active wear that's going to get filthy. I do believe in buying good quality though because of the amount of times you're going to wash this stuff. Nobody cares what you look like in your workout clothes; feeling good and being comfortable is all that matters.

I have five pairs of trainers because I wear them for different styles of training. For bootcamp, I wear Gore-tex waterproof trail trainers because they are the ultimate pair of outdoor trainers. They are waterproof and I thank God that somebody designed them as I really need them in this English weather! They also grip mud and grass too. They are a really great buy. There is nothing worse than having cold, wet feet hours after you have finished working out. You need a different style of trainer for pavement running. Any good running shop will have a whole selection of styles/makes and price ranges to suit your needs.

When I ran the marathon, I had to drive fifteen or so miles to the nearest running shop to buy a decent pair of running trainers for me. I wanted to go on one of those running machines and have a specialist fitter tell me the best ones for me to buy. They are not just a trainer. If you are going to spend money on one piece of active wear, I would advise that footwear is the most important. That doesn't mean they have to be expensive, just be sure they are good quality and right for the style of training you do. You also have to take into consideration that pavements and grass become slippery when wet. Good grip on whatever surfaces you might be training on is essential as far as safe training is concerned.

Some trainers out there are purely designed for fashion, not sport so make sure you do your research before you buy. Go to a reputable sports shop and tell the assistant exactly what you're buying the trainers for and they will point you in the right direction and they should make sure the trainer fits you properly. The sizes in different brands vary. I may be one size in one brand and another half or a whole size different in another trainer brand. This is what makes buying them online so tricky unless you're 100% sure of what you want and what your size is in that particular brand of trainer. I have had to send trainers back countless times. It can be frustrating. I allow a side on thumb between the tops of my toes to the top of the trainer to be sure of a correct fitting for me. I have suffered a few times with blisters and black and lifted toenails due to poorly fitted trainers. It's painful and off putting, it can also put a stop to your training for a few days whilst your poor feet are recovering.

- **Sports socks** - Come in a variety of types; long, short, ankle, blister resistant which are a little more expensive but can be worth it.

- **Sports Bras** – There are many on the market and I would suggest trying them on until one fits. When I see women running down the street without one on I think ouch that must be uncomfortable. I always wear two sports bras; one which is a normal bra designed for sportswear that fits me well and a stretchy, elasticated crop top style sports bra that goes over the top. Wearing two bras ensures everything stays where they should be. I will jump up and down to be doubly sure of that. Just be sure to take off the top one if you're not working out as it can feel quite restrictive and get a little hot under there.

- **Leggings** - Your actual workout gear is not as much of an issue. As long as you're comfortable and it fits you properly. There's nothing worse than leggings that you have to hitch up because they are falling down. Also be aware of camel toe. To avoid this, there are some styles that you need to steer clear of. Go for the diamond shape of material that's sown in on the crutch piece. It's another reason I will not buy online unless I've tried on an equivalent exact same pair in a shop but they just don't have my size to buy there and then.

- **Tops** - Your sports tops should be fairly tight if you do floor work as your top tends to rise up so unless you're prepared to tuck it in to your bottoms it may rise up. Not what you want for modesty's sake more than anything.

- **Shorts** - I'm seeing men now wearing leggings under their shorts in the winter. Great idea.

- **Jackets** - If you're training outside especially in the winter times then you need to stay warm and dry. I find more thin layers are better than one or two thick layers. It doesn't take long to get warm. In a five minute bootcamp warm up you go from freezing cold to boiling hot in no time at all. At least with lighter layers you can strip off and tie them around your waist or put them in a rucksack. Waterproof Sports Jacket - Is a must if you're working out outdoors. They don't tend to be very warm though so I will wear my thin lightweight padded jacket underneath. A waterproof cap is a very good buy. It not only helps to keep your hair dry and out of your face, it keeps the rain out of your eyes so you can see where you're going.

- **Gloves** – I can't bear having cold hands so I have both waterproof winter sports gloves and fleece ones for the colder months. I've also got a fleece neck scarf tube; they are usually worn for skiing but are perfect for outdoor sports in the winter time too. If my neck's cold, I'm cold. If you have the right gear, you will feel far more prepared for the task in hand. It should make you feel good to stick on your workout gear. It's the norm to wear your workout gear all day now which is illustrated by the amount of people you see going about their daily lives while wearing it. Larger supermarkets also tend to sell sports gear now, as well as nearly all department stores. You will not be stuck for choice. There are so many nice brands out there so find one that you can afford.

There is a lot of specialist sportswear available in the market that I haven't included such as tennis, golf and swim wear. Use the internet to find your specialist sportswear retailer as close by to you as you can. Be sure to wear reflective clothing if you are out in the dark running/walking or on your bike as it's always best to be seen. Be safe be seen.

"Happy long, active life, equals LONGEVITY"

10

Longevity

I love the word longevity. The definition of longevity is 'A long individual life; great duration of individual life: Our family is known for its longevity. The length or duration of life.'

Longevity is the very good reason why you have to look after and take good care of you. What's going to help you get longevity? Optimal good health and a positive outlook on life are going to help you attain it and keep it. Your diet is the most important part of this with exercise being a close second. Surround yourself with people you love and do the things you love doing. I wouldn't want my longevity to be any other way. Your life is completely your responsibility. Once you get this in your mind it really is all in your hands as to how your future will unfold.

I think when you're young you just don't think about growing old. It's too far away in the distance and it feels like it will never happen to you. It comes around so much sooner than you think. I cannot believe I'm nearly fifty; how did that happen so quickly? Looking back on my life though, I can clearly see the good choices I have made and the steps that I have taken to get me to a point where I am happy with my life, today. One of the biggest reasons I wanted to become a personal trainer was to teach people how to become fit. I wanted to show people how they could incorporate fitness into their daily lives, as I have done. I call myself a fitness trainer rather than a personal trainer as it's all about the fitness for me. Helping clients to achieve the body and the healthy lifestyle they want. I want to help my clients work out safely and effectively. I want to pass on my passion for exercise in order to motivate and inspire other people to make the same changes that have empowered me. It gave me the life I wanted to live, the life I'm living now. I have designed a life I am happily living. I'm proactive in my life and know I will always be this way. I am a work in progress always working on and improving being me.

From observing my own grandparents growing old, I am able to see the bigger picture. My paternal grandad Fred told me his biggest regret in life was smoking as this habit nearly killed him and he suffered from COPD in his retirement years. He was looking forward all his working life to his retirement years, where he should have been able to enjoy his golden years but could not. This condition he had brought on by smoking robbed him of that chance. COPD is short for chronic obstructive pulmonary disease; it's a lung condition brought on by smoking. This disease caused my grandad to have emphysema and he would suffer from bronchitis which got worse during the winter months. He had to carry oxygen around with him and would grow tired easily. He really wished he hadn't smoked or at least not have smoked for as many years as he did. He smoked for most of his adult life and only gave up when he was told if he didn't he would be dead within a year. It was horrible to see him suffer; especially knowing it was so preventable. There are many other illnesses linked to smoking. Smoking will NOT help you to live a healthy, long life.

I used to work as a care assistant looking after the elderly and clients with debilitating illnesses who were unable to care for themselves. I have seen with my own eyes what happens when we grow old and we have not looked after our bodies when we are younger. Having to have somebody come into your home to care for you because you cannot do it yourself is no quality of life. That's not what I want for myself or for you. I believe as we grow older we should speed up not slow down. To counteract our muscles diminishing, we should work against this urge to slow down. The older lady that crossed the finish line with me knew better. Running her eighteenth marathon in her seventies should show us all what can be achieved later in life.

Another older woman who I'd like to pay tribute to is Earnestine Shepherd. She is my exercise hero and I want to be just like her when I grow up. Please google her if you've never heard of her. She showed me that the quality of life and health you have in later years is determined by the daily choices you make right now. There is a picture of her online standing next to a typical eighty year old with white hair, hunched over a walking stick. Earnestine is holding a kettle bell and her body is toned and amazing; especially for somebody in their eighties.

The more you give in to slowing down and becoming inactive as you get older, the more inactive you will become. The decline occurs; the more you sit around the more you will want to sit around. You'll stop going out. You will resign yourself to being stuck indoors at home. You will sit for longer periods of time stuck in front of your television using the remote control. Then you get a remote controlled chair to lift you out of your seat. A stair chair to take you up to your bedroom. By making our lives easier, we are actually letting ourselves become lazy and inactive. I am not destined to grow old and be stuck in front of the television screen, no thank you. Remember the advice I gave at the beginning of this book? The big secret in life is you have to spend energy to get energy. That applies to your whole life. Do not give in to fatigue. Rest sure. Keep it moving. As you get older, continue to exercise, focusing on your core to counteract muffin tops and beer bellies. The middle aged spread. You will also find getting out of your chair and bed will be much easier. I have seen people really struggling to get up off the floor. You've got to keep that core strong as it supports your spine. All of your upper and lower body movements come from your core (that's your stomach muscles) I advise all of my clients to increase the amount of work they do on their core muscles as they get older. This is why you have to make exercise an integral part of your life. Becoming old and inactive will ensure you lack good quality of life. You will kick yourself when you are older for not doing all of this when you had the time. It does go back to it's never too late for change. Always remember that.

It's also important to think of our children and the message we are sending them. If our children see us being active and looking after ourselves it stands to reason that they will also get into this mind-set from a young impressionable age. Then they will want to follow suit. We must lead by example. It's been an important part of my journey for my children to see how I respect my health and love my body. It also helps them with their self-image when they are bombarded on TV, social media and the internet with images of what they 'should' look like. Being a mother of teenage girls I have tried my best to build up their self-esteem and let them make their own choices of how their bodies should be. I haven't wanted to tell them what to do, I just wanted to guide them into making good, healthy choices.

Obesity is a massive problem worldwide now, and it's cutting our lives short. We are eating way too much of the bad food. It's so easy to eat badly now with takeaways and eating out. It's no wonder we're getting obese when we can click a button on our phones and have a pizza delivered to the door. In the U.K alone 1 in 4 adults aged sixteen and over are obese. This is going to shorten your life expectancy and potentially make you ill. The problem isn't just with the health issues either. This obesity is also the reason why so many people are unhappy with their bodies. If weight is the reason you are unhappy with your body then only you can change that. Don't complain and feel bad about it. Be proactive and do something about it. Flick that mind switch. Instead of thinking about what you have to give up, think about and focus on how good you will feel and how you want your body to represent you. It's about respecting your health and your body. You need to take control of the situation and stop eating those unhealthy foods in order to be happy with your body. Eat the healthy foods. You're not depriving yourself because you're still eating. Only you have the power to change and it's very much in your control. Make it happen. It took me a while to enjoy drinking green tea but now I love it because of all the benefits. I never used to enjoy vegetables, yet now I am a vegetarian. The same with exercise. I once didn't enjoy any of these things, but look at me now. I now enjoy all of these things because they are good for me. It's the circle of good. Do good - good comes back to you.

You can become addicted to almost anything in life. Make sure it's a good addiction; swap your unhealthy addictions for healthy addictions. Whenever I've wanted to stop doing something I've found a way to give it up and replace it with what I do want. It goes back to my second chapter Mind; it's very much MENTAL. The body won't go where the mind doesn't take it. Open your mind to change.

I hear a lot of young people say they feel old and I'm not surprised, because it is what they are telling themselves. I, however, am 49 years young! You will never hear me say I feel old because I do not. Everything I do is keeping me looking and feeling younger and so I am young in my mind and in my heart. My body follows suit.

If you know me personally you will know that dancing is one of my favourite things to do. Once I hit the dance floor it's hard to get me off. I've been like this since my early twenties and I'm still going strong. Music is a big part of my life it is a great mood changer I so enjoy working out to good music. It's kind of like dancing for me. I have been known to break out into a dance mid bootcamp. I just cannot help myself.

'You don't stop dancing because you grow old, you grow old because you stop dancing!' How true is that? You're only as old as you feel and if someone tries to tell you any differently remember once again, it's their limited belief not yours. I plan to dance and laugh my way through the rest of my life. There's nothing more heart-warming for me than to see older people enjoying a boogie on the dance floor. I assure myself, that will be me one day. Enjoy every moment of your life. Never restrict yourself with an age limit. You're a long time dead. We have to live our lives to the full; we owe it to those who did not get the chance to live to be older. Enjoy your life to the maximum. Party on people.

I know yoga will keep me younger for longer. I've heard good things about Pilates as well. Yoga makes you more flexible and supple so it means that your body doesn't feel older it feels younger. I'm as flexible now as I was in my early years. If you see a person that's older that does yoga you will see how their posture is really good and how they just seem to hold themselves with grace. Jennifer Aniston is a big yoga fan and she looks awesome. Yoga improves your balance, stability and coordination which all very much decline as you grow older. It wasn't until I did yoga that I realised that just the simple act of yoga breathing could bring about so many benefits. We seem to forget that breathing keeps us alive as it's just something we automatically do and we just take it for granted. There's so much more to it than that. I have used my yoga breathing many times to bring me back to the present if I feel myself getting anxious. Before

I went out on stage to take part in the bikini fitness contest I felt my legs turning to jelly so I focused on my breathing.

You quicken your breath or even hold your breath without realising when you're feeling anxious and this makes you feel even more anxious and can bring on a panic attack and make you feel faint. If you can slow your breathing down, take a nice deep breath using the count of five, and then exhale on the count of five, five times over, you can make yourself calmer. I tried it with a friend recently before a flight. It worked perfectly. At that moment on stage, it bought me back to reality so my mind wasn't racing forward and I was able to get my legs back under control. I then calmly walked onto the stage and did what I had gone there to do.

Just learning to do breathing techniques will help you so much in your life. I have learnt this not only with yoga but also for public speaking. Doing that contest was a big stepping stone for me to get me into public speaking. I'm actually quite shy, or at least I used to be. I'm very confident now and this is because I took this stepping stone of stepping out on stage wearing a bikini. Once I'd done that, I knew I could definitely get on a stage and talk whilst fully clothed!

It was all about taking the little steps to get me to where I want to be. I seem to have done things back to front, but that's ok there's no hardened rules to the game of life. It's all happening as it should be.

I monitor my thoughts and feelings a lot. If something makes me happy I do more of it and if something makes me unhappy I try to do less of it. It's the same with gut feelings. I have read that our brains, gut and heart are all very much connected. I will ask myself lots of questions and then stay silent for a while and the answer will come to me through thought. We all have this ability but unfortunately because of television and other life distractions we tend not to hear ourselves think. I'm very much in tune to me. I know what I want. I know what makes me happy. If I'm happy then my body is happy. I do everything I can to be sure I am happy.

Everybody wants to be happy and it's yours for the taking. Own your happiness; it comes from within. Know your mind, know yourself. Make the right choices in life and you will be the happy you and have the happy body that you want. Embrace change and be open to it. Something that brings me so much happiness is helping others; we rise by helping others. It's something I've always loved doing even from a young age.

We all have the same amount of hours in a day. There's one hundred and sixty eight hours in a week. If you work 9-5, 5 days per week that's forty hours. We sleep on average 8 hours per night. That's fifty six hours. That leaves you with seventy hours per week. How could you not have time for exercise? Even one hour per day is just 7 hours out of your seventy. If you look at it like that, knowing what you know now, what are you going to choose to do with your time?

Slow steady progress is what you should be aiming for with your fitness and in life. Think tortoise and the hare. If you are persistent you'll get it, if you're consistent you'll keep it. And once you find what works for you, keep doing it. Congratulate yourself for the little achievements as well as the big ones and give yourself a clap after every workout; I do. Everybody loves praise. Remember to focus on the big picture rather than the short term. At thirty, I knew I wanted the energy to run around after my children and also that I wanted to be fit and healthy enough to run after my grandchildren and great grandchildren.

Since I turned forty, I have had two over forty health check-ups at the doctors. The last one I had was at the age of forty seven. The check-up consisted of a blood pressure test, weight check and cholesterol test. I also answered a series of questions. When the results came back, the nurse told me I was the healthiest 47 year old on her records. I was only marked down one point from the available one hundred and this was because I drink more than the recommended units in a weekend it can be labelled as binge drinking. I'm working on drinking more water and less alcohol to correct this. I have to take responsibility for my actions and do something about it. I hear many people complain about the NHS but I praise it, as we are so fortunate to receive the care that we do. I've only got good things to say about them.

You will make mistakes along the way but hopefully you learn from them and remember; nobody's perfect. I stopped blaming everyone and everything else and took control of my own life and I've never looked back. I have found out what I want in life by trying everything and saying no to the things I know I don't want. Life is a learning curve. Stop procrastinating and take action. I believe that you can do it.

I learned meditation through doing yoga and this has bought calmness and peace to my life. I'm learning about the seven chakras in the body of spiritual energy. I have discovered in recent years that I am spiritual. I probably have been all my life but just didn't know what it was. I do see things differently than most. Inner peace means a lot to me, as does peace on Earth. I fill myself up with love. I give it back out to the world. The more I love then the more things I find to love; there's no room in my heart for hate. The more I love the happier I become. Through reading and researching and making good choices I have found a solution that works for me and I very much hope that by way of reading this book I will have helped you to have the right tools and work out a way that will work for you too.

It can start from a tiny seed of inspiration and grow like that. Taking up running - Signing up and running the marathon simply started out as a thought and I followed it through. Look where that thought took me. All off of the back of running the London Marathon and discovering so much about myself. My fitness journey has led me to writing a book and becoming an author. I can now add writing a book to the list of goals that I have achieved. Where will your fitness and taking care of yourself take you I wonder?

Remember; impossible becomes I'm possible.

Think it - Believe it - Action it.

Make it happen.

Dear reader,

Thank you for reading my book. I hope you enjoyed reading it as much as I enjoyed writing it for you. I wasn't sure at the beginning of my book writing quest how I was going to do it as I've never written a book before. I just knew that I would. I have to say that it all fell into place as if it was meant to be.

From the moment I made the decision to write a book, I met all the right people to help me to put this book together and I made it happen. I had no idea how to do it. Like everything else I want to do, I researched and asked questions. I went on a book writing course and educated myself as much as I could to help you. When it's not about you and it's about helping others I honestly believe you can do no wrong. I have tried my best to write this book to help you the best I can.

Fitness is most definitely the way forward for everyone. Young or old, male or female; it will add so much value to your life and to those around you. Be authentically you. The world needs more of that.

Not everything in this book will be for you, but I'm hoping that there's something for you to think about; even if it's a tiny seed of fitness inspiration. Take from it what you will.

If something in this book has resonated with you then I would love for us to continue this journey together. If you visit my website you can arrange a Free Consultation with me, as well as try a Taster Session at one of the Happy You, Happy Body Bootcamps. Here's the link:

www.HappyYouHappyBody.co.uk

I'd love to see you grow into your awesome self and step into your own "Happy Body". To be comfortable and confident with who you are, happy in your own skin. Become your own happy ever after and keep *looking after you.*

I would love to know how you get on after reading this book and if it has helped you in some way; even if it's accepting yourself the way you already are. Please feel free to email me any feedback or questions on hello@happyyouhappybody.co.uk

Best wishes for your healthy, happy future and a 'Happy You, Happy Body'.

Much Love,

Karen Jones
Fitness Guru

"The Happy Body Creator"

Alternatively you can connect with me via social media on:

f *Happy You Happy Body*

⊙ *happyyouhappybody*